CW00368952

Waterskiing

Paul Seaton & David Emery

Waterskiing

Faber & Faber · London & Boston

In the same series
COMPETITIVE
JUDO
by George Glass
RALLYING
by Chris Sclater
and Martin Holmes
TABLE TENNIS
by Harold Myers

First published in 1978 by Faber and Faber Limited
3 Queen Square London WC1
Set by Filmtype Services Limited, Scarborough
Printed and bound in Great Britain by
Redwood Burn Limited, Trowbridge and Esher

All rights reserved

© Paul Seaton and David Emery, 1978

British Library Cataloguing in Publication Data
Seaton, Paul
  Waterskiing.
  1. Water skiing
  I. Title   II. Emery, David
  797.1'73   GV840.S5
  ISBN 0-571-11325-7
  ISBN 0-571-11222-6 Pbk

Contents

Foreword

BY LORD WAKEFIELD OF KENDAL

As civilization evolves and standards of life improve so do the opportunities for a variety of leisure recreations increase. Moreover the tendency of people is to participate in those recreational activities which can best be enjoyed by both sexes and by families upon more or less equal terms. Waterskiing satisfies such conditions. For obvious reasons waterskiing has been a late starter.

However, because of the enjoyment given the increase in the numbers of people participating has been phenomenal. By nature man is competitive and there is of course the innate desire always to improve and become better and better in the quality of achievement.

No one is better qualified than Paul Seaton to explain how to achieve quality because it was to that end that he dedicated himself and in so doing achieved much personal success and a great deal of satisfaction. In waterskiing the improvement in skills has been rapid and a great deal of knowledge has now been acquired. It is very desirable that this knowledge be communicated widely.

This objective is admirably achieved by Paul Seaton in his book. Waterskiers will enjoy their sport the better if only they will take the trouble to read this excellent book which should be closely studied.

Wakefield of Kendal

President of the British Water-Skiing Federation

Foreword

BY MIKE HAZELWOOD MBE

I am delighted to recommend this book to all waterskiers, no matter what their age or ability. Paul Seaton was the finest male waterskier ever produced by Britain until his tragic knee injury cut short his career in 1975 just as he stood on the threshold of the world championship.

It is typical of his courage and his deep love for the sport that he has continued to share his wealth of knowledge both as a coach and as author of this excellent guide.

Paul was always a tremendous competitor, the one they all had to beat. I skied with him from the age of fifteen and know that part of my success now is directly due to his influence. He is a model for any skier – and one who really does know what he's talking about. As this book will prove.

Mike Hazelwood

World Champion 1977

Very special thanks to

my parents
Rainer Kolb my trainer
Haileybury College for extraordinary privileges

also thanks for financial support during my skiing career to

The Winston Churchill Memorial Trust · Leisure Sport ·
The British Water Ski Federation · The Daily Telegraph · University Motors ·
Typhoon Wetsuits · Fletcher International Sportsboats · Ace Crash Helmets ·
Powerboat and Waterskiing

We are grateful to the following for permission to reproduce
photographs in which they hold the copyright: Francisco Bedmar ·
Tony Duffy / Allsport · Colin Taylor Productions · Raymond Thatcher

and thanks to Patricia Roskilly who did the line drawings

and thanks for complimentary or subsidised training to

Princes Club · Jack Travers International Tournament Skiing, Florida, USA ·
Jim McCormick's Ski School, Florida, USA ·
Liz Allan's Training Camp, Florida, USA · Club Lorraine, Nancy, France ·
Vanersborg Klubb, Sweden · Muurame Kerho, Jyvaskyla, Finland ·
Yarrawonga, Victoria, Australia · Ruislip Club ·
Shangrila Club, Ohio, USA · Thorpe Water Park

1 *Introduction*

Tell somebody you are a waterskier and they immediately think you vote Tory, live in a detached, five-bedroom house and pass the odd weekend in Acapulco.

Waterskiing, along with hunting and shooting, is filed under the heading 'rich man's sport'.

Well, maybe that was so a few years back, but now waterskiing is within reach of almost everyone in the British Isles. More and more clubs are buying their own boats and loaning skis and most seaside operators will provide a worthwhile session for a couple of pounds.

Nor is waterskiing the province of just the fit and the brave. I have helped coach a fourteen-month-old baby boy, skied regularly with a seventy-year-old fanatic and watched a labrador dog cruise serenely over the water in Miami, Florida, hanging onto the tow rope with his teeth.

There is nobody in the world, given basic health, who cannot waterski. Some of them just take a little longer than others.... If you are the type who has a few bob to rub together and can afford your own boat, the smallest you should buy is one with a maximum speed of about 25 mph (40 km). That ensures there is enough power to get the average size skier onto the water. Beginners always need more impetus than experienced skiers because they are more inclined to plough through the water.

If you don't own a boat and have no boat-driving friends, pick out a coastal operator or a ski club. There are more than 120 clubs in Britain and a list of names and addresses is available from the British Water Ski Federation, 70 Brompton Road, London, SW3 1EG (telephone: 01-584 8262).

All you need to start with is a swimming costume and a bit of nerve. Most clubs have a selection of skis, starting from as small as 30 in (75 cm) for the tiniest tot through to 70 in (180 cm) boats for the well-fed business executive.

The length of ski suitable for you depends on your weight. I am 165 lb (75 kg) and the ideal length for me is about 65 inches (170 cm). The scale roughly goes like this: Junior (up to 120 lb/55 kg): 50–60 in (125–150 cm); Adult (120 lb/55 kg upwards): 60–70 in (150–180 cm).

The longer the ski the broader it becomes, like the base of a raft to support the load. It is important you find the correct size: too large creates difficulties manoeuvring, too small makes it hard work.

Land practice

The first stage is learning the correct stance on land – without skis and without the rope. The position is normal and natural:

1 Stand square.
2 Feet 12 in (30 cm) apart.
3 Knees bent.
4 Back straight.
5 Arms straight out in front of you.
6 Head up looking straight ahead.

There should be no crouch and no hunched shoulders; just a totally natural stance. The knees are bent to help balance and act as shock absorbers. The surface of the water is constantly changing and flexed knees help ride over the contours without upsetting the rest of the stance.

To start with, do not use your hands or arms during the land practice. They are, after all, only the means of attaching the ski line to the skier, so for now keep them down by your sides and concentrate on the leg movement.

Sink down into a crouch position, balancing on your toes. Keep the back straight and head up. The knees must be parallel, not splayed apart. If that happened in the water you would fall forwards.

From the crouch position, stand up very slowly, straightening onto the toes and then transferring some weight on to the heels. It's just like getting out of an armchair. Repeat many times until the movement is fluid and natural.

Then you are ready to use the hands and arms with a ski handle. And this is probably *the* most crucial of all exercises for the learner skier – and the most frustrating for his instructor. The arms *must* be held straight and never bent. They are the locking device which joins everything together. But the most common fault among novices is the completely natural, reflex action of bending the arms to haul themselves onto their feet. It is always a short cut to disaster on the water, sending the skier crashing out of control (as will be explained later).

There is a little trick which overcomes this problem

Hold the handle with your palms down, which is the standard grip for all beginners. Now twist out – hard – with your hands and your arms will be locked in a straight, rigid line.

Keeping the arms in that position continue the land practice as before with someone holding the rope. The rope must always be slack so that the skier has to use his legs only to stand up. If it is taut he will pull himself up on it – a situation which is impossible once he gets in the water. If the person holding the rope feels a big tug, he should let go of it and allow the skier to fall backwards – that will drive the point home.

Equipment

The next stage is to get used to wearing the equipment – life jacket and skis. A wet suit is also advisable.

The life jacket must fit snugly round your body, otherwise it can ride up around your neck and head and become most uncomfortable. A ski belt is a smaller version of a life jacket and I consider it a very inferior safety aid as it would do little to keep your head above the water in the admittedly unlikely event that you took a heavy fall and knocked yourself unconscious. But it is better than nothing and I must stress that no beginner should attempt to waterski without wearing one of these aids. The sport, at a fun level, is mercifully free of accidents and we want to keep it that way.

To put on the skis, first wet your feet and the bindings. The bindings are adjustable rubber pouches which should fit snugly like a tennis shoe, but not tightly. When you take a fall, you want the ski, not your foot, to come off. Also you will have to put the skis on while floating in the water and that will be almost impossible if the bindings are too tight.

Bend over the ski standing up, place your foot into the bindings toes first, raise your heel slightly and then with both hands grasp the heel of the binding and pull it on as you press down with your own heel. If you use only one hand you are likely to finish up with your heel in a lopsided position.

Still on the land, sit back on the skis with your knees fully bent and your chest resting against them. Keep your arms out straight and round the *outside* of your knees. Your skis will have a tendency to splay as you stand up once you get in to the water. Placing the arms around your knees will hold the skis together. As you rise the arms will automatically come above the knees. Now, with someone holding the tow rope, simulate the pull which will bring your weight on to the balls of your feet (Fig. 2). Then stand up as before.

Figure 1

Figure 2

Into the water

Never have your skiing baptism in rough water – it is difficult enough without that. And if it isn't too cold practise taking your skis on and off in the water before settling down for the ski proper. All water movements must be done slowly and with the minimum of fuss, otherwise you will become flustered and waste energy.

Figure 3

For the start, sit back on the skis as you were on the land. You will be unable to actually touch the skis with your buttocks because the skis will sink backwards in the water. The front tips of the skis should be just out of the water, about 8 in apart and with the tow rope between them.

You will find the skis difficult to control in the water the first few times. They tend to float up and to one side. If that happens, roll over onto your back again, bend your knees up to your chest and pull the skis up in front of you. Test the position a few times before involving the boat driver. But once you have mastered it and are settled, sit still . . . and relax.

If you are tense and nervous you will rarely get up first time. The aim is to come out of the water slowly and smoothly. If you move quickly you throw yourself off balance.

You should establish a language with the boat driver consisting purely of 'Yes' and 'No' to start with. 'O.K.' can be confused with 'No' over a distance and other words are similarly distorted. So when you feel ready to begin, shout 'Yes'.

The boat should be driven at idling speed as it draws the skier through the water to give him time to gain control. Some of the cowboys operating around the Mediterranean give an almighty whoosh on the throttle and the skier explodes from the water. He usually explodes straight back again because his balance is shot to pieces.

Simply increase the speed like a quality car pulling away from traffic lights when the skier is completely set and all will be well.

The first sensations might well be unpleasant for the skier. As you are dragged, crouching behind the boat the water may well rush up your nose, into your eyes and wash out your mouth. Hang on . . . the experience to come will be worth it.

Remember – do not attempt to pull yourself up with your arms in any way. The boat weighs a ton, so it is quite capable of lifting you onto your feet. Bending your arms will bring you up too quickly, make your skis shoot ahead of your body and send you falling backwards. Allow yourself to be pulled out of the water in the crouched position, with your knees bent and your weight on the balls of your feet. Once you feel secure try and stand upright by using your legs only – as on the land.

When you have managed to stand up – still keeping the knees bent – the tendency will be to lean forwards with your back rounded. This is an uncomfortable position as well as being incorrect, so try to straighten yourself by pulling backwards with your waist (Fig. 5). If you stay in this bent position too long you will grow accustomed to it – and these early habits die hard.

Don't worry if the skis wobble around a lot, that is only natural. And make sure that each manoeuvre is performed *slowly*.

There are two useful hints which may help you get up into that correct position:

Figure 4

Figure 5

1 Shorten the rope from its standard 75 ft (23 m) to about 40 ft (12 m) before you start. That way you can talk with the boat driver more easily.
2 If your skis repeatedly splay as you try to get up, bind them three or four inches apart. It's not cheating – just a way of helping you enjoy yourself.

In America they have devised the ingenious method of fitting a scaffold pole out from the side of the boat, giving the skier total support. The driver has to be skilful on turns, though, otherwise the pole lifts and its occupant is skiing on air. Properly used, it is an ideal way to teach children, which is an art all by itself (see page 21).

Falls

Falls will be the rule rather than the exception as you learn to ski. Never be discouraged by them. The average person takes about five attempts to get up on his skis for the first time. I took eight.

But having said that, some people have a tendency to fall too easily. They start to wobble, think it is all going wrong and let go of the handle. Hang on until you really are falling, you will be surprised how many of these shakes you can cure.

As you progress up the scale you will be doing yourself a disservice if you do not fall regularly. It will mean you are not testing your ability to its full potential.

Your life jacket will absorb most of the impact of a fall. Just relax when you feel yourself going and try to roll over on to a shoulder.

Because the boat circles back to you after a fall, you will probably end up with the rope trailing around you. For safety's sake flip the rope over your head and let it run through your hands. If the rope is wrapped around your body and the driver accidentally accelerates away you can end up with a bad rope burn.

Time limit

Do not stay on the water for more than four or five minutes for your first couple of skis. You will be discovering all kinds of new muscles and these need to be built up steadily.

Hand signals

Hand signals are a vital language between skier and boat driver. The most commonly used are: thumbs up: 'more speed'; thumbs down: 'less speed'; thumb and index finger joined in a letter O: 'everything O.K.'; hand flat down on head: 'take me back to the jetty'; finger across throat: 'cut throttle'.

The most important of all is the clenched hands raised above the water to signify all is well after a fall. Raising one arm means the same, but I feel this can often be a reflex action. Always raise two arms and clasp the hands – then there can be no mistake.

Edging

Once you have mastered the technique of getting on to your feet you will want to turn corners with the boat. To do that you simply bank the skis by leaning slightly in the direction you wish to turn. The inside edges of the skis will bite the water and you will automatically move into an arc. This is known as 'edging'.

Crossing the wake

The wake is the pair of waves left by the boat's track through the water. It can expand for as much as 30 ft (10 m) when the boat is moving slowly to as little as 6 ft (2 m) when the boat is travelling at speed. The wider the wake, the higher it will be and a large ski boat moving at 20 mph (32 kph) will push out a wake 18 in (45 cm) high.

When you feel competent on the skis you must learn to cut across this wake. It takes quite a bit of balance and determination and there are a number of weekend skiers who have never attempted it. But it is an essential step if you wish to enjoy the full thrills of waterskiing. To cross the wake you must learn to edge decisively and push down more with one foot than the other. As in snow skiing, you push down with the foot opposite to the way you want to go. Push down left and you turn right, push down right and you turn left. The harder you lean the more you will edge and the faster you will traverse.

Weave around inside the wake at first and then to negotiate the wake build up momentum by edging and keep the knees bent to absorb the sudden bump. Grit your teeth as you set off. Apprehension will only earn you a ducking.

As you progress sharpen up your angle across the wake until you are cutting as near to right angles to the boat as possible. You are now ready for mono-skiing.

Mono-skiing

The Americans call it the threshold to skiing – and I cannot disagree. Everything is heightened – the thrill, the speed, the strength of turn. As the old saying goes, if you don't want to be hooked on waterskiing, don't move on to one ski.

You will have to make two vital adjustments:
1 Grip 2 Position of arms

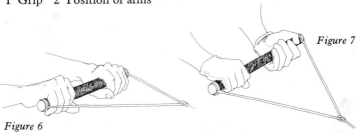

Figure 7

Figure 6

Grip Instead of the palms down grip (Fig. 6), you must now change to the 'one up one down' method (Fig. 7). Hold the handle with your left palm up and your right palm down. Not the other way round – even though you may see champions using it. The reason for doing it my way is that 'left up, right down' is the way you must hold the handle for jumping when you eventually come to tackle it, so it is as well to learn that way now rather than having to swap around later on.

Arms Lower the arms to waist level, but still keep them straight. This will bring the pull down from chest height to waist level, the centre of your body, and give you a far greater degree of balance for the testing exercises ahead. Later, you should also bend your elbows slightly so they can act as shock absorbers against slack in the tow rope, but you are not that advanced just yet.

Choosing your mono-ski

Never use a slalom ski when learning to mono-ski. A slalom ski is designed for faster, harder and deeper turns and at this stage will hinder your progress. Instead use an ordinary pair, preferably with one ski fitted with two bindings for mono-skiing.

Lifting a ski

Now you must decide which is your stronger skiing leg. Lift each leg in turn as you go along until you are certain which leg you prefer to ski on. Being right or left footed has nothing to do with it. I am right footed but always ski on my left leg.

To lift a ski and give what is known as 'the skier's salute' (Fig. 8).

Figure 8

Slowly transfer your weight on to the one leg and gradually lift the other ski off the water, forcing your toes up as you do so. Should the tip of the ski dip into the water the back will swing up under the pressure and deliver a sharp admonishment to tender regions. You will also fall.

Test your new ability by repeatedly crossing both wakes with one ski raised. Lean into the direction you want to go and the ski will automatically edge. You are bound to fall a few times during this stage but once you have mastered it you are ready to join the élite on a single ski.

Moving on to a mono-ski

The mono-ski has bindings for both feet. The rear binding is merely a ridge of rubber like a slip-on shoe. What you have to learn to do is to slip it on while being towed behind the boat.

Wear the mono-ski on the leg you have decided is your best for skiing. Loosen the binding on the other ski because that will be discarded once you are on the water.

When you feel well balanced on the water, transfer all your weight on to the mono-ski. Press downwards with the toes of the foot you are freeing and lift the heel out of the binding.

Keep the toes pointing down, brush the ski backwards, and slowly lift the leg clear of the water, allowing the ski to drop away. Never kick it away, that will upset balance. Bring the free knee up towards your chest and tuck the foot under your buttocks. Then freeze until you are settled again. Slowly run the foot down the back of your skiing leg until your toes reach the ski. Feel for the back binding and push your toes back beyond it and then slide them forwards into the binding. The aim is to get the foot flat on the ski with your weight equally distributed through both legs. If your ski has no back binding, simply place your foot flat on the ski with the toes touching the back of the front binding. This is sufficient for now, but you will have to find a mono-ski to progress any further.

A lot of people ski with their back heel up. This is purely because they have too much weight on their front foot. Usually it also means their body is all bent up and they have little chance of ever tackling a slalom run properly. It is essential you get both feet flat on the ski so the weight is even.

You will find the single ski has a tendency to wobble. Keeping the knees bent will help it track smoothly.

Ensure the ski moves as a single unit by locking your back knee into the socket provided by your bent front knee.

Practise your single-ski technique by traversing the wake; shallow turns at first becoming progressively harder until they are as near to right angles to the boat as possible. After the first few traverses, you should start bending the elbows a little so that the arms can now act as shock absorbers.

Deep-water start on one ski

When you are tired of dropping skis all over the lake (the nearer the start the better, incidentally, both for safety and to save time) you are ready for the deep water, single-ski start. The news will bring a smile of relief from your boat driver who has had the job of retrieving all those discarded skis – although in some ways you are probably about to test his patience more severely. For, make no mistake, this is the hardest procedure you have yet come across and I defy anyone to get it right the first time.

There are two ways of tackling it:

1 With both feet in the ski.
2 With one foot in the ski and the other trailing.

There is no right or wrong. But I favour the one-in one-out method because it is easier.

It takes a lot more effort from the skier and a lot more throttle from the boat to get up on the water with both feet in the ski. Balance is so delicate and there is more drag because all of you is pointing in the same direction.

On a more trivial level, if you have both feet in the ski and both legs pointing in the same direction, you are more likely to get a jet of water up the leg holes of your wet suit.

With one foot out, that trailing leg acts as a balancing weight. Stretch it as straight and as far out behind you as you can and it will act as a second ski, helping you by pushing down on the water.

Squat in the water with your buttocks resting on the heel of your front foot, your chest bent forwards and the front leg bent upwards as much as possible. Arms slightly bent to take the pull. Keep your bodyweight over the ski by leaning forward a little with the shoulder on the ski side. The tip of the ski must be clear of the water – and by 'tip' I mean all of the curved part of the ski. This allows the ski to come clearly up onto the water and not plough through it. The rope, of course, has to be held on one side of the ski while you are waiting for the pull. Which side is entirely your choice; there is no correct procedure – just the side which feels more natural.

I favour holding the rope to my left side because my left foot is forward and I have a tendency to be pulled that way as I start off. By holding the rope that side, it rubs against my ski and acts as a railway line to keep me straight in the water. It is only a momentary thing. The rope rises above the ski as soon as you break through onto the surface.

There are two rules which must be underlined again and again for this start: stay down; stay back.

Stay down   Don't be in a hurry to get up. Come onto the water in a crouch and wait until the boat has sufficient momentum to pull you up easily. Otherwise you will just bury the tip of the ski under the water and fall forwards.

Stay back Keep that trailing leg back as a stabiliser until you are certain everything is as it should be and bring the shoulders back as you stand up to ensure the tip of the ski remains out of the water.

As the pull comes, use your free leg as a rudder. If you start to go one way push down with it and steer in the other direction. Do not push down with the ski, that only creates more drag. Just let the water bring you up. And as you start to rise, use your shoulders to balance your weight in such a way that the ski tip follows a path directly under the line of the rope.

There are various other starts you can try:

Shallow beach start or 'Scooter' start

This is ideal for coastal areas. The water should be just below your knees and no shallower. Stand on your free foot with your ski out in front of you. The front tip should be a couple of inches out of the water with the back of the ski angling down under the water. Drop the shoulder the same side as the skiing leg so that your weight is over the ski. Bend your knees, arms and back a little to take the sudden shock of the pull.

Hold the handle with one hand and a couple of coils of rope with the other in such a way that they can run free without trapping a finger. The coils will act as your 'go' signal. As the last one unwinds grab hold of the handle with that hand as well. Keep the line to the boat straight by pulling on it as the coils start to unwind – otherwise when the pull first comes it will be off to one side.

The boat must have plenty of power for this start so that the initial momentum is enough to pull the skier directly onto the water in an almost upright position. Use your trailing leg as a balance and an extra rudder. Beware not to anticipate the boat's pull and step onto the ski before the rope tightens. You will sink.

Sitting dock start

Sit on the dock facing the stern of the boat with your shoulders braced and slightly forwards. The ski should be in the water at an angle of about 30 degrees with the tip a couple of inches clear. Hold the coils of rope as in the 'Scooter start' and keep the arms down ready to take the pull at waist level. Your free foot hangs loose ready to drag through the water as an extra ski – or if there is a handy ledge, to give you an initial push off. (The procedure is the same in principle for beginners on two skis.)

Standing dock start

This is the ultimate start – good for show, but not so good for the ski. I broke one in half once coming off a fairly high dock, so it can also prove expensive. There are two ways to stand for this:

Either you grip the dock with your free foot like a diver would and hang the ski over the side with the tip angled up. Or you stand on both the ski and your free leg and, as you jump off, push the ski out in front of you and angle it upwards. If you have fine balance the first method is probably easier for you; but the second is more commonly used.

The boat needs plenty of speed to hold you up as you plop over the side and because of that, judgement of the coils is critical.

Traversing

The purpose of skiing on a single ski, of course, is as a build up to slalom skiing. The serious skier should always remain acutely aware of his next objective – and the means of achieving it.

In this case, that means single-ski traverses across the wake as tightly as possible – and these introduce you to the glorious intricacies of acceleration and deceleration.

Acceleration – edge with pull. Deceleration – edge without pull.

Try a series of fast, but smooth, turns about 15 ft away from the boat's wake. That means accelerating across the wake, decelerating for the turn and accelerating away again to get in position for the next turn on the side of the wake.

Starting from your usual position behind the boat, the way to do it is this: pull hard across the wake to your right, leaning and edging as much as possible. Change edges as you come out of the wake and lean to the opposite side. The more you edge, the more you will decelerate, but the aim is to get a smooth, progressive turn. Your lean should increase as you turn and be at its most acute at the end of the turn. Increasing lean – decreasing arc and that tightness of turn is crucial when you move to the slalom course.

Accelerate out of the turn, across the wake and then change your edge and decelerate into the opposite turn. At no time should you be on a flat ski, that will cost you braking power and make you late for the turn. A flat ski should be merely the transitional split-second between one edge and the other.

There are a couple of easy guidelines to help you determine the merit of your turns:

1 If your deceleration is insufficient you will find yourself holding a few feet of slack rope.
2 The spray should be smooth and crescent-shaped as you make your turn. If it is jagged your turn is erratic.

Returning to the jetty

The way to return to the jetty is not to time it as fine as possible before letting go of the handle. A few people have miscalculated and come to a messy end. Let go in good time and be prepared to swim a bit.

Never aim directly at your landing point. Ski parallel to it. As you let go of the handle crouch a little on the skis to compensate for the loss of pull. If you are travelling too fast sit back on the skis and drag your hands through the water.

Teaching a child

Teaching a child to waterski is like teaching your wife to drive. Patience and tolerance are everything. In most ways the procedure is the same as for an adult, but the following hints should make the task easier:

1 Make sure he wants to do it. Waterskiing is supposed to be fun and bullying him will only make him more temperamental and less likely to succeed.

2 Eliminate as much of his fear as possible by talking to him gently. Reassure him by explaining why he won't drown when he falls, why he won't hurt himself, why the boat won't go fast.

3 Give him a life jacket, never a ski belt. If he doesn't believe it will keep him afloat take him into the water and prove it.

4 Find as calm and quiet water as possible – and preferably waist-deep only. Children lose their nerve very easily.

5 Judge the tightness of his ski bindings yourself. Children are apt to complain that they are too tight or too loose when they are perfect.

6 If the bindings are too loose, let him wear socks or plimsolls.

7 Make instructions simple and limited. Children are usually keyed up and will forget long, elaborate orders.

8 Be certain he remembers the most important procedure of all – 'Clenched hands' after a fall.

9 Ensure he is conducting his land practice with straight arms before putting him on the water. If there is even a hint of a bend continue to drill him thoroughly.

10 Correct any fault – either on land or water – immediately. Children, in their excitement, find it hard to forget bad habits.

11 Emphasise that the boat will do the work – 'it's bigger than you are'.

12 Pull him a long way with the boat idling and do not increase the power until you are certain he is completely steady.

13 If he is very young and you are competent, ski in the water with him. Otherwise let him do it for himself – that way he will be less reliant.

14 Reassure him when he falls – children have delicate egos.

15 Give him only four or five attempts the first time if he fails to get up. Children become disheartened very quickly and will start to detest the sport if they feel they are failures.

16 If all else fails, put him on an aquaplane. This is similar to a surf board attached directly to the boat. He can do what he likes on it with little fear of falling off. It will give him a sense of balance – and the thrill of the ride. And that is what it is all about.

2 Slalom

Mike Hazelwood, muscles bulging and cheeks puffing, portrays the concept of slalom

Slalom waterskiing at its highest level is among the most exhilarating of all sporting experiences. Your reflexes, timing and, most important-ly, technique are put under searching scrutiny as you reach speeds of more than 80 mph (130 kph) and G-forces of about 500 lb (225 kg).

With that kind of pressure to contend with, it is imperative that you

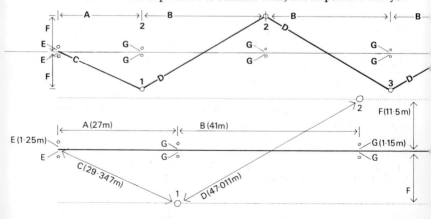

have a thorough knowledge of the basics. It can be a painstaking business progressing step by step up the slalom ladder, but I cannot stress too strongly the importance of patience.

The skier who, at his first attempt, yells 'hit it' to the boat driver and goes hell bent towards the buoys is taking a short cut to disaster – and it could cost him his nerve. Where there is speed, there is also an element of fear; the good skier overcomes that fear by a gradual build-up of confidence.

The slalom course

The regulation slalom course is 285 yds (260 m) long by 25 yds (23 m) wide with an entrance gate, six contestant or turning buoys and an exit gate. The first buoy is on the skier's right, the last on his left.

The boat travels down the centre of the course through a lane marked by six sets of guide buoys opposite each contestant buoy plus the entrance and exit gates.

The dimensions of the slalom course are agreed by the World Union and should be constant everywhere. In fact, they are inclined to vary slightly because of the obvious difficulties in laying out the course. The World Union has agreed to a degree of tolerance and competition skiers should give every course they tackle a thorough check in practice.

Rope lengths and speed

In competition, the skier starts with a tow line of 75 ft 5½ in (23 m). If he enters the gate, makes all six turns round the buoys without falling and goes out through the exit gate, he has completed a 'pass' and the boat speed is raised 2 mph (3 kmph) each time to make the next pass more difficult.

Once he reaches the maximum boat speed of 36 mph (58 kmph), the tow rope is progressively shortened with each successful pass. From that 75 ft 5½ in (23 m) it decreases like this: 59 ft 10½ in (18·25 m) 52 ft 6 in (16 m), 46 ft 9 in (14·25 m), 42 ft 8 in (13 m), 39 ft 4½ in (12 m) and finally 36 ft 11 in (11·25 m). Skiers tend to refer to these reductions as '15 off', '22 off', '28 off', etc.

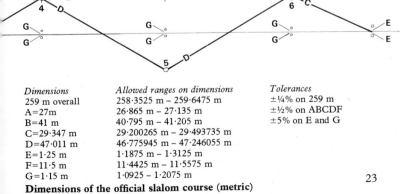

Dimensions	Allowed ranges on dimensions	Tolerances
259 m overall	258·3525 m – 259·6475 m	±¼% on 259 m
A=27m	26·865 m – 27·135 m	±½% on ABCDF
B=41 m	40·795 m – 41·205 m	±5% on E and G
C=29·347 m	29·200265 m – 29·493735 m	
D=47·011 m	46·775945 m – 47·246055 m	
E=1·25 m	1·1875 m – 1·3125 m	
F=11·5 m	11·4425 m – 11·5575 m	
G=1·15 m	1·0925 – 1·2075 m	

Dimensions of the official slalom course (metric)

Kris la Point (USA) working his arms to the maximum

The shortenings are the same for women, juniors and dauphines. But the maximum boat speed for women is 34 mph (55 kmph). Juniors and dauphines have the same maximums as adults.

A timekeeper in the boat decides if the correct speed has been attained. It takes 17·0 seconds to go through at 34 mph (55 kmph) and 16·1 at 36 mph (58 kmph). A tolerance of two-tenths of a second either way is allowed at 36 and three-tenths at 34. If the boat is too slow, the judge will order a re-run.

The timekeeper should check his watch at the third buoy of each run to ensure that the driver is not going fast into the course and slowly out – or vice versa. The speed must be constant.

The beginner will be ready for the slalom course when he feels totally at ease zigzagging across the wake with plenty of lean. But the first thing he should do is step out of the water and take a long, appraising look at a good slalom skier in operation on the course. That way he will get a feel of what he has to attempt and that mental picture will be translated partially to his limbs.

He should be aiming for a smooth rhythm, not heave and pull with brute strength. The slalom run is there to be enjoyed and mastered, not fought like an enemy.

Stance

The stance is exactly as for mono-skiing and you should ensure that the knee of your back leg is resting in the bend of your front knee. That way the legs will be locked as a unit, as an extension of the ski, not operating independently and harming balance.

A few years ago the style was to work the legs independently – and some ski manufacturers still follow this school and produce slalom skis which keep the feet some 8 in (20 cm) apart. For the modern, locked, method the feet should be no more than 2 in (5 cm) apart.

It is important to remind yourself again that the legs should be flexible with the knees bent to absorb the shock of the wake and water. The only other part of your body which needs to move during slalom are your arms and head. By leaning the body you will make the ski do the rest.

The boat speed on your first run should be as slow as possible and by that I mean just enough to prevent you from sinking. I know this will be highly unpopular. As you have progressed with mono-skiing you have obviously upped the boat speed and been delighted with the newly found power and comfort. Skiing at speed is so much easier.

Well, sorry, but the only correct way to learn slalom is to revert to snail's pace. About 22 mph (33 kmph) is enough for most people although I have gone as low as 15 mph (24 kmph) with children.

If the speed is too high you will lose control and it is essential in slalom that you are always performing within yourself in the early stages.

Now, forget all about the entrance gate. The No 1 buoy is the hardest and most critical on the course anyway so there is no point complicating matters by trying to go through the gate correctly as well. That will follow soon enough. For the time being just try to get round the first buoy in as good a shape as possible. This is how to do it:

Pull out to the right of the boat until you are wider than the first buoy. Aim to clip the back of the buoy as you lean round it in a graceful arc on the left edge and then take the boat's pull to power you across the wake towards buoy No 2.

A lot of beginners have trouble here. They pull to the first wake, relax, and then pull after the second wake. Apart from giving them a

Figure 9

Peter Bryant (GB) almost brushing the back of the buoy

jerky, inconsistent action, this also cuts down on their power and means they will be arriving late at Buoy No 2. There should be a good steady pull across both wakes. In fact, because you are going so slowly you will have to pull until you are almost on top of the buoy. There is little need to decelerate for the turn because you will slow down automatically.

Aim above the buoy, never at it, change the edge, finish the turn and pull back across the wake. You should be leaning back with your shoulders to keep the weight at the rear, body straight, knees bent, and most importantly, your arms down around hip level. It is very easy to allow your arms to go out in front of you but if that happens there will be nothing to absorb the pull of the boat and you are likely to be yanked forwards off balance. Keep both hands on the handle at all times. The single-handed turn comes much later.

Although you have ignored the entrance gate, always ski through the exit gate. This is nowhere near as difficult. Missing it out is pure laziness – and creates bad habits.

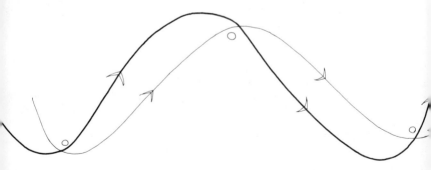

————— *Skier using correct line aiming above the buoys*
——— *Skier aiming at the buoys and losing space*

Slalom beginner

Bruce Cockburn of Australia caught with his arms out and buckling under the strain

△ *Liz Allen Shetter (USA) shows her aggressive style as she rounds a buoy*

Mike Suyderhoud, American world champion, is obscured by the clouds of his own mistakes after a ferocious hook turn, but determination prevails ▷

▽ *The author turns contortionist as he hits problems*

A lot of instructors teach that beginners should ski *inside* the buoys to get the feel of the slalom course. I totally disagree.

The skier is already experienced with traversing – as skiing inside the buoys would be; the aim now is to get used to the width of the buoys and the pull necessary to get round them.

Also, skiers become used to taking this easy way out and inadvertently do so when the pressure is on in competition. Slalom skiing is all about guts and determination, being bloody-minded enough to really want to get round that next buoy. It is tragic the number of good skiers one sees opting out of a buoy when, with a little more effort, they might even have gone on to make a complete pass.

If you want to get anywhere in competitive slalom skiing you need to develop this killer instinct from the start. The true joy is to discover the limit of both yourself and your ski.

Half and quarter buoys

These are the fractions which win high-level tournaments. They are of little consequence to the learner – except for the inner satisfaction which he will receive from trying that bit harder and pushing his score up bit by bit.

The way to calculate whether you have scored a full, half or quarter buoy is shown in this diagram.

The skier gains a full buoy when he turns a buoy and reaches the wake, a half buoy when he crosses line *A* and a quarter buoy when he crosses line *B*.

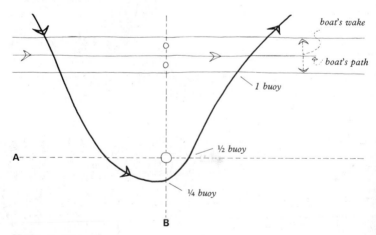

Half and quarter buoys

When you have successfully negotiated the course a few times at crawling pace you can start increasing the boat speed. But only by 1 mph each time – you will be surprised at the difference it makes. I

The author approaches the buoy . . .

at full reach . . . and accelerating hard out at the end of a perfect turn

Sigi Schneider (West Germany) has lifted her free arm and is suffering the consequences

The author receives a powerful blow on the hip from a slalom buoy

have known skiers to be perfectly happy at 24 mph (40 kmph) and make a hash at 26 mph (43 kmph). It seems ridiculous, but it's a fact.

So don't rush it. If you are falling, or missing the buoys repeatedly early on in a run at 24 mph (40 kmph), reduce your speed and start building up again. This is no time for false pride; mistakes compounded now will be that much harder to eradicate later.

As the speed rises so you will begin to look more and more as if you are skiing across the water rather than being dragged through it. At about 26 mph everything should start to take shape properly – and that's when you are ready to tackle the entrance gate. This is largely a question of trial and error as you learn to judge speed and distance. You must progress little by little, gradually getting wider and wider to the left of the boat before you start your initial cut in across the wakes. It is at this stage, also, that you can start attempting to make your turns with one hand only.

There is a lot to concentrate on because this is the hardest of the three waterskiing disciplines to perfect. Ideally, though, you should go through the course in the following way:

Study the course as the boat approaches it. You need a decisive mental picture of what you are going to attempt. Pull out to the left of the boat about 50 yds (45 m) from the entrance gate. This needs to be timed accurately; if you go out too soon you will lose speed and drop back, too late and you will get slack rope because you can't slow down in time.

Come almost to right angles with the boat, holding onto the handle with both hands. You will see quite a few champions using just one hand at this stage but it takes a split second to replace that other hand and you may not have the time to spare if you have made the slightest misjudgement.

Make a relaxed, easy turn and then pull powerfully and smoothly to and across both wakes. Aim to almost clip the inside of the right-hand gate buoy to give yourself as much space as possible to get wide of the first contestant buoy.

As you approach and cross the wake you are accelerating on your right edge. As soon as you have crossed start changing the edge so that about 20 ft (6 m) beyond the wake you are already starting to decelerate on the opposite, left, edge. You should never be on a flat ski in slalom.

Changing the edge brings you smoothly to the start of your turn which should be the shape of a decreasing arc. You are trying to clip the back of the buoy. The nearer you can go without actually hitting it, the better. I often used to finish training sessions with my thighs and arms covered in red weals from where they had smacked against the inflated plastic balls.

As you start to turn let go of the handle with your right hand. This gives you better balance, better reach and helps use up slack rope when you put it back on the handle and pull in. Keep the hand down by your side during the turn – not up in the air as that causes the body to arch.

Extend your left arm and the handle towards the boat and parallel with the water. As you come to the final part of the turn the ski will

33

point momentarily towards the boat. That is when you start to accelerate out again by bringing the handle in and grabbing it with your right hand. The hand and handle should meet halfway. If you reach forward to take it you are more likely to be caught with your arms out and tugged off balance. Also, by bringing the handle back to meet your hand you are taking possible slack rope.

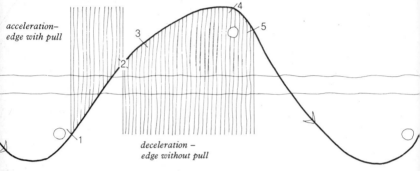

*acceleration–
edge with pull*

*deceleration –
edge without pull*

1 *Acceleration begins*

2 *Start changing edges; deceleration begins*

3 *Ski is momentarily flat; release one hand*

4 *Skier begins to bring arm in and place second hand on handle*

5 *Corresponding to 1; arms in, full lean*

NOTE: i *The exact location of the various points naturally changes slightly with different rope lengths.*

ii *Acceleration and deceleration in distance travelled are approximately equal, but in distance down course (space) very different*

Slalom skier's aim

You must take the pull in a powerful position: arms in, body back, knees bent. The rope will be stretching under the intense pressure and the whiplash effect will catch you out if your stance is wrong.

Ski hard over on the left edge and accelerate powerfully out of the turn towards the wake. Cross both wakes leaning and pulling. Start changing your edge as you come over the second wake and decelerate into buoy No 2, releasing the handle this time with your left hand.

Calculating how much power you should put into the pull across the wake is the most crucial test of all. You must, of course, have sufficient thrust to carry you wide of the buoy and enough impetus in hand to allow positive deceleration. But it is pointless blasting flat out across the wake and then having to put the brakes full on in a desperate, last-second attempt to get round the buoy. Speed without strain is the name of this game.

Judge each buoy carefully and separately. A lot of skiers treat slalom as routine, pulling and deceleration in exactly the same spots no matter where they are skiing. Remember, all courses and boat drivers differ fractionally. You should always be viewing the next buoy and adjusting your skiing accordingly.

The author shows the correct dynamic angle of attack after the turn

△ *Italy's world champion Roby Zucchi still pulling and leaning as he crosses the wake*

▽ *. . . he approaches the second buoy in world champion style*

John Arthur (Scotland) is setting his sights on the next buoy even while completing this turn ▽

Even experts have problems . . . Sylvia Terrachiano of Italy ends up with a mass of slack rope

he bugbear of the slalom skier. Slack is inevitable the more
ress because it becomes increasingly difficult to decelerate
enough. Slack must be absorbed with the arms, back and knees
otherwise it will pull you off balance. This is why smooth turns are so
important; a steady, controlled turn will use up some of the slack, a
ferocious turn breeds it.

Short-rope slalom

Short-rope slalom is a psychological barrier more than a physical one
in the early stages. Of course, it is harder to reach the buoy because you
have less rope, but the technique involved in doing so is easier because
the initial pull is more powerful and direct towards the next buoy.

The shorter the rope, the more staccato the pull, until at the later
shortenings it is a real snap which makes your veins bulge and muscles
crack if you aren't in the correct position to receive it.

But although the pull is shorter in time, the distance covered on the
water remains the same. So the lean, edge, acceleration and deceleration phases must be cleaner and sharper.

There are three important points to remember for short-rope slalom
especially, even though they apply equally to long-rope slalom.

1 As the angle of the pull increases, the head and shoulders tend to
open towards the boat. This must be resisted and the body kept square
to the ski.

2 The pull requires far more effort than the turn. Some skiers relax
their pull after the initial acceleration and throw themselves into a
full-blooded, energy-consuming turn. This makes for jerky, fatiguing
slalom. Put most of your power into the pull, accelerate across the
wake, and then make the turn smoothly and easily. A smooth turn also
puts you in position to take a powerful pull.

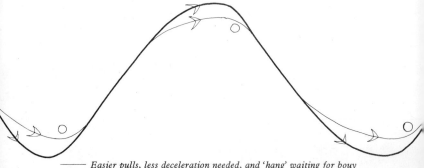

——— *Easier pulls, less deceleration needed, and 'hang' waiting for bouy*
——— *Harder pulls, more deceleration and harder needed. Precise judgement.*
Two different methods for the short-rope expert

Karen Morse (GB) makes the turn with ease but is poised for the pull

3 The major part of the ski must be kept in the water. This gives the resistance so necessary for efficient acceleration and deceleration. If you come out of a turn on the heel of the ski, you will get good speed but no bite and will lose direction and be dragged down the course.

There are two ways of tackling the problems posed by short rope.

1 You switch on full power and aim to heave yourself wide of the buoys through speed and strength.

2 You regulate your pull, approach the buoy at a narrower angle and sharpen up the end of the turn.

In theory, the first method is best because it allows more space for the turn. But in practice, the degree of judgement for the acceleration and deceleration is so critical that it achieves only limited success. The second method allows a far higher margin of error. You need not commit yourself so early as you are, in effect, waiting for the buoy to come to you.

△ *John Battleday (GB) takes the pull and shows the effort required*

▽ *Mike Hazelwood waits for the buoy with perfect form and line*

The success of your slalom depends entirely on the co-ordination between speeding up and slowing down. If you are late for buoys it is because you are not pulling hard enough. To regain your rhythm you may have to hook turn round the buoy – and this is the only instance when you force the turn with a sharp, powerful flip. Do not overhook, though, or the ski will skip out.

If you arrive at a buoy with a lot of slack it is because you are pulling too hard or too long. Some top skiers dip their handle in the water to aid deceleration – this is unorthodox and should be used with caution.

There are three small don'ts:

1 Don't lower the boat speed to get the feel of a new shortening. The whole point of shortening the rope is to give greater speed and a stronger pull.

2 Don't jump the wake. It only wastes vital split seconds which would be better spent edging.

3 Don't jump through the entrance gate. Keep your ski in the water otherwise in competition the judges may think you have missed the gate and you could be disqualified. I speak from experience.

Turning

It is a physiological fact that the skier who stands with his left foot forward on the slalom ski will turn better to his left and vice versa. This is because the pull for a left turn comes more down the left side of the skier's body and into his front leg naturally and comfortably. When he turns right the pull comes more down that side of his body and has less natural 'feel'.

The left-foot-forward skier, therefore, should have an advantage because the most crucial buoys on the course are Nos 1 and 5 – both left turns.

A good No 1 is vital to set the skier right for the entire course. No 5 is important because psychologically it is the last buoy you have to get round. If you get a good turn at No 5 it doesn't seem to matter in what shape you take No 6: you invariably survive to cross the exit gate.

I say the left-footed skier 'should' have an advantage because at the highest level this is not usually so. The right-footed skier, conscious of this apparent disadvantage, practises endlessly on his weaker side while the left-footed skier, blithely believing he has been heaven-blessed, does little to improve his turns at buoys 2, 4 and 6.

I am a left-foot skier and guilty of that awful complacency. I now know it to be a terrible weakness for top-class skiing. I can even remember times when I was in great shape at 1 and all over the place by 3. It was as drastic as that.

In fact, it cost me dear in the world championships at both Bogota and Banjolas. Both times I fell on the third shortening at No 2 when to have survived that run would have put me in the final.

On the other hand, my strength with the left turn won me my first European title at Temple Sur Lot, France, in 1972. I desperately wanted to win and was so nervous I was skiing timidly. I knew I had to make the third shortening in the final to give myself a chance of the overall title against the Italian Robbi Zucchi and Max Hoffer, but because I was so tense I was making bad turns. I came round 4 in terrible shape but knew that if I could reach 5 I would be able to put it all right. I got there, used my good turn to improve miraculously, made 6, the exit gate and the title.

It was rough water that day which was another reason I was successful. In fact, all three of my European overall titles were won in the rough. This is largely because I always made it a point to train in bad conditions. A lot of top Americans shun rough water, refusing to train in it for fear of spoiling their style. But 80 per cent of the ski venues around the world are susceptible to these conditions and if you have no experience of them you are at a grave disadvantage.

By rough, I mean water where you feel your performance is hindered by excessive waves caused by wind or backwash. Really smooth water can be almost as tricky because the ski is prone to skid. A bit of chop helps deceleration.

Rough water

For rough-water skiing I recommend you stick to your usual ski. A longer ski with hard flex will give a slight advantage in the conditions but it is outweighed in my opinion by the comfort of familiarity. I had a short ski which I used for all types of slalom and it was excellent in the rough.

The technique is to increase the pulls and slow down the turns. A turn in the rough will render the ski far more likely to skip out of the water.

The correct stance is imperative. It is easy to let the arms be pulled away from the body by the extra stresses and that can be fatal. If you hit a wave and your shock absorbers are gone, so are you. Knees well bent, of course. The ski will be wanting to bounce about all over the place and only bent knees will hold it steady. Keep your weight back, a little more so than usual. If you hit a wave with your weight forward you will come over the ski. And being back keeps the ski biting in the water. Some skiers are timid about leaning in rough water. In fact, it is important that you work the edges harder than usual. On edge the skis will slice the waves instead of bouncing over them.

Headwind, tailwind, sidewind

Headwinds aid deceleration in slalom skiing because they automatically slow you down so a longer pull may be necessary.

Tailwinds hinder deceleration so you may have to force your lean and pull less strongly.

The author completing a turn harder than usual to make up lost time

Sidewinds are the trickiest of them all because you must use a different technique on either side of the course. Going into the wind your pull will have to be longer and your deceleration area shorter. With your back to the wind the pull will have to be shorter and the lean stronger.

Physical advantages

It is an obvious help to be tall for slalom skiing. Those extra inches give that bit more room for manoeuvre when the rope starts shortening and longer legs absorb the shock of the wake more. But the taller and heavier skiers also exert more pull on the boat and some drivers cause them problems by overcompensating.

But no matter what your size, when you have run a slalom course and get the chance of competition, have a go. I managed exactly half a buoy in my first tournament yet it was a wonderful thrill.

And remember: If you have been skiing at 28 mph, don't start off at that speed if you have the option to start slower. Build up stage by stage to give yourself the feel of the course – and the confidence to go on and win.

The author in trouble with slack rope and the handle in the water . . .
amazingly he recovered

3 *Trick skiing*

Trick skiing is the most challenging and, in my opinion, most enjoyable aspect of the sport. It is open to the widest range of people because you can get by with smaller boats and shorter stretches of water. It is also, unfortunately, the hardest to learn.

You will fall countless times, be frustrated repeatedly and probably feel like chucking it all in. Persevere – that pain in the neck will become the joy of your life given time.

Trick skiing is entering an exciting new era, with standards improving by staggering proportions each year. Already there are some 120 possible tricks to be learnt – and the certainty of many more to follow.

Trick skiing favours the smaller, more compact person. Most of the great trick skiers like Suarez, Stiffler, Cockburn, Stehno and McCormick have low centres of gravity. The taller skier tends to be less agile.

Grip

Revert to the palms down method used when you were learning to ski. If you use the one-up one-down grip for trick skiing the handle will twist away from you when you turn on the skis. When you are skiing backwards to the boat, the palms are up.

Figure 10

Stance

1 Bend knees.
2 Skis about 4 in (10 cm) apart.
3 Back and upper body vertical with slight kink in waist.
4 Arms in and held at upper hip level.
5 Majority of weight on the balls of the feet.

Skis

Shorter (about 40–42 in (100–105 cm) on average) and wider (up to 30 per cent of the length is permitted). Light for ease of control and finless to allow them to slide.

A fair amount of time should be spent skiing normally to get used to the very different feel of the skis. Do plenty of traversing especially, and practise hopping over the wake.

Boat speed

Set the boat speed at a comfortable level. This will vary from skier to skier, depending on his size and ski size. But the majority will settle for somewhere between 15 and 20 mph (24 and 32 kmph). The larger the ski, the slower the speed will need to be. If it's correct you will not skid over the surface nor feel bogged down. Insist that the driver gets it right – and keeps it constant.

Rope

Shorten the rope from the beginning. A lot of people teach that you should start off trick skiing on a long rope because the water is calmer the further back you go from the boat's propellers. I disagree for two reasons:

1 The closer to the boat you are, the better the wake's characteristics. You will be performing many tricks with this wake before long so it is as well to get used to being near the boat from the start.
2 The shorter the rope the less time it takes to put the skier back on the water after one of those countless falls.

Between 30 and 50 ft (10 and 15 m) of rope is enough depending on the characteristics of a particular boat's wake and your speed. Ideally, at this stage, the skier should be about 5 ft (1·5 m) from either wake when he is in line with the centre of the boat.

There are nine cardinal points which the skier should be aware of when learning tricks:

1 Look up at all times. If you drop your head the entire upper body tends to follow. As the saying goes, look up or you will go down.

Slack rope is inevitable . . . even for world champion Maria Victoria Carasco (Venezuela)

2 Keep the arms in and down from the start to finish of a trick. The rope will become slack at times as you twist and turn and it is imperative that the arms are in to act as shock absorbers when it snaps back. Keeping the arms down automatically lowers the centre of gravity and means you are taking the pull in the place most helpful to your balance. I always tried to concentrate more on this point than any other in competition because I found that if I had this right everything else fell into position.

3 Keep the back straight. This enables you to pivot on a near vertical axis and keeps your weight centralised on the ski. The lower body slopes fractionally towards the boat, bringing a slight kink to the waist. This ideal position will also be the most comfortable.

4 Keep the knees bent and flexible. This is the most important point for ski control. The skis have no fins and therefore will not track effectively unless you use your knees. Even in advanced trick skiing straight legs are the most common mistake.

5 The majority of weight should go through the balls of the feet. As on land, much more balance can be achieved through the balls of the feet rather than the heels. This is the key to agility, which, in turn, is the essence of trick skiing.

6 Keep the skis close together. If they are allowed to spread the edges will catch as you attempt a turn. Also, the closer they are the more compact you are.

7 Never throw the handle from one hand to the other during turns. Always make sure you are holding it with one before you let go of the other. This is a common mistake with advanced skiers and one of the main reasons for falls.

Always pass the handle – never throw it, as James Carne (GB) is now remembering

8 Aim to turn gently. The more explosive your turns the more likely you are to blow yourself off balance. Turning gently makes it easier to stop at the end of the trick – and therefore cuts down the interval time between that and the next trick. All the great trick skiers make it look calm and effortless.

9 Judge the top of the wake correctly. This is imperative with all wake turns. If the skier calculates correctly he can use the ridge of water as a kind of springboard for the turns and not need to jump at all.

Nor should the skier cut hard at the wake – that has three disadvantages:

1 It becomes more difficult to judge the top of the wake.

2 Travelling at the faster speed lessens control.

3 The impetus carries the skier further away from the wake and increases the time before the next trick. Those lost seconds are vital in competition.

Turning too soon is a common mistake and often ends in a fall because the ski edges knife into the top of the wake and create drag. The skier also loses the full effect of the wake springboard, jumps to compensate and forfeits balance.

Two other points for wake tricks: Firstly, as I have said, you should not need to jump if you judge the wake correctly. You have only X amount of effort to put into each trick and if you expend it all leaping into the air you will have none left for the turn. But if you *still* find you have insufficient height for a clean turn spring from the knees *only* in a kind of bunny hop. Otherwise the jump will cause motion in the upper body, again upsetting balance. Also if you do not need to jump, your knees will automatically remain bent for landing as they should be.

Secondly, the formation of the wake is such that the elevation is normally sharper when you come into the wake than when you go out from it. Skiers should use this greater thrust and generally learn high-degree turns going from outside to inside the wake first.

Memorise these nine points above. Then, every time you fall or fail with a trick, run through them like a checking chart and you should be able to analyse each mistake. Be careful, though, not to overdo it. Too much analysis and soul-searching will make you tense and relaxation is a keyword in tricks.

There are two main categories of tricks: surface tricks and wake tricks. Surface tricks are performed, would you believe, on the surface of the water; wake tricks are performed moving across the wake and clear of the water (the turn is away from the centre of the wake when you approach from the inside and towards the centre of the wake when you approach from the outside).

The amount of turn, or spin, involved in a certain trick is described in degrees. Thus a half turn is a 180, a full turn a 360 – and so on.

Skiers never seem sure of the order in which they should learn

The author completing a wake step back to front on two skis with plenty of height and yet no signs of jumping

tricks. The simplest, and best, method is to follow their competition points value. Every trick is awarded a certain score when performed in tournament and it follows that the trick with the smallest value is the easiest to learn. (A complete points chart is provided later in this chapter.)

By using this method you also know the exact point to start learning one-ski tricks as well, i.e. when the points value for one-ski and two-ski tricks become identical. Even the simplest one-ski trick carries good marks and it is pointless spending hours learning difficult two-ski tricks which you will never use in competition.

Figure 11

Skiing backwards

Up to now all your skiing has been done going forwards. As you progress in trick skiing you will be called upon more and more to ski backwards. So it is important that you practise this unnatural position. Try plenty of traverses in and out of the wake until you are confident.

Normal and reverse

All tricks have a normal and a reverse turn. 'Normal' means the way which you favour, i.e. a left-foot-forward skier will have a normal turn to the left when he is skiing forwards and to the right when he is skiing backwards. The 'reverse' is the opposite turn. The execution of these turns is usually identical, so the reverse turn will be described in this chapter only when it differs from the normal. In competition, the normal and reverse are always performed consecutively because the rules state that if they are performed independently the second one will not count.

Jean Veys (Belgium) in perfect backward position on one ski

Wrapping and hand-to-hand

These are the two ways of tackling high-degree wake turns such as 360s and 540s where you have limited time and need a lot of spin. 'Wrapping' means winding the rope around your body before you start the trick so that the pull of the boat automatically spins you out.

It is an ideal way of learning the trick but time consuming in competition where every split second counts unless used at the very start of a run when you can 'wrap up' outside the course. That is why the more experienced skier uses the 'hand-to-hand' method which, as it suggests, means moving the handle from one hand to the other as you turn.

I would suggest that the only tricks to learn on two skis are the basics – side slides, 180s, 360s – and then wake 180s, wake 360s, steps and wake steps.

When you have mastered these, concentrate on one ski. Your time will be more profitably and enjoyably spent. The advanced two-ski tricks are often harder to master than their one-ski equivalents – and they are 'one-off' tricks, not helping in any way towards learning a subsequent trick.

I believe all except the steps should be learnt in normal and reverse – and it is very important that you practise the two versions simultaneously. Do not master one and then move to the other. As in slalom, every skier has a preferred turn and if you learn only the turn you favour you will become a very lopsided trick skier.

Once you are past the stage of learning the basics on two skis, make sure you are always working on several tricks at the same time. Variety stimulates interest. And before you tackle each new trick, try and imagine yourself doing it, concentrating on those nine commandments listed earlier.

Don't be afraid to try a difficult trick, especially if you get a sudden urge to do so; you might be surprised how close you get. Carlos Suarez, the Venezuelan world champion, learnt his tricks back to front by mistake, starting with the hardest and becoming progressively easier!

Land practice

Generally speaking I am against land practice for trick skiing. Water is constantly on the move and I feel it is impossible to simulate the same conditions on land. Trying to do so can often breed mistakes. For instance, if you try to imitate a 540-degree wake turn on the land you will need to spring very high and hard to get the necessary elevation. On the water the wake provides a natural ramp, as I have explained earlier. But if you have been practising on land you will have convinced yourself that you need to jump hard despite the wake and you will constantly be throwing yourself off balance.

Land practice is fine to get the feel of single tricks and sequences merely by stepping through them – or to get the idea of where the rope and handle will go, particularly during a wrap. Otherwise it should be discouraged.

A trick pulley is a useful aid because the weights simulate the pull of the boat.

One-ski tricks

A lot of people find one-ski tricks easier because they don't have to worry about the other ski waggling around and possibly catching in the water.

Stance Your better leg forward, as in slalom, but this time with the back foot at an angle of 45 degrees (Fig. 12). The majority of your weight

Figure 12

Description	No.	Water turns 2 skis Basic	Reverse	1 ski Basic	Reverse	No.	Wake turns 2 skis Basic	Reverse	1 ski Basic	Reverse
Side slide	1	20	20	70	70					
Toe-hold side slide	2			150						
Wrapped toe-hold side slide	3			230						
180 Front to Back	4	30	30	60	60	15	50	50	80	80
Back to Front	5	30	30	60	60	16	50	50	80	80
360 Front to Front	6	40	40	90	90	17	110	110	150	150
Back to Back		40	40	90	90	18	160	160	210	210
540 Front to Back		50		110		19	240	240	310	310
Back to Front		50		110		20	250	250	320	320
720 Front to Front		60		130		21	400	400	400	400
Back to Back		60		130		22	430	430	430	430
900 Front to Back						23	550		550	
Back to Front							550	550	550	550
180 F–B stepover	7	80	80	120		24	110	110	180	
B–F ,,	8	70	70	110		25	110	110	160	
360 F–F ,,						26	200	200	260	260
B–B ,,						27	200	200	260	260
540 F–B ,,						28	300	300	420	420
F–B ,,									500	500
720 F–F ,,									480	480
540 B–F ,,						29	300	300	420	420
B–F ,,									500	500
720 B–B stepover									500	500
180 F–B toe-hold	9			100	100	30			150	150
B–F ,,	10			120	120	31			180	180
360 F–F ,,	11			220	220	32			300	300
B–B ,,	12			250	250	33			330	330
540 F–B ,,	13			350	350	34			500	
720 F–F ,,				450						
540 B–F ,,	14			350		35			500	
180 F–B toe-hold stepover						36			320	
B–F ,, ,,						37			380	
360 F–F ,, ,,						38			450	450
Forward somersault						39	500		500	
Backward somersault						40	450		450	

Trick values

Franta Stehno (Czech) European trick champion in classic toe-hold position

should be through your front foot. When you perform a trick that makes you ski backwards to the boat, maintain the kink in the waist and your weight will automatically be slightly away from the boat to counteract the pull.

Toe-holds

Toe-hold tricks are those executed with the handle held by your foot (Fig. 12). They are as difficult as they sound. Possibly the hardest part is learning to put your foot through the handle in the first place. Keep your weight forward on the ski, bend both legs as normal and very slowly raise the other leg up towards the handle. Bring the handle down to meet it about 18 in (50 cm) off the water. This part is critical – if you lift your foot too high you will fall backwards, if you bring the handle too low you will fall forwards. Make the strap grip by pulling back your toes with the knee bent. That knee is now the shock absorber. To release the handle just point your toes forward. Test this position with plenty of practice skiing, especially to and fro over the wake.

When you start attempting toe-hold reverse turns, make sure you have someone competent looking after a tow-rope release mechanism on the boat. The toe reverses are dangerous tricks and should be attempted only when skiers are fresh and fit. The release mechanism, which drops the tow rope instantaneously, is not necessary for other toe-hold tricks. Tow releases take a lot of time to re-attach and on normal toe-hold tricks the worse that can happen is for you to be dragged behind the boat for a few yards. A loose toe-strap will prevent that – as well as providing a guide to your proficiency at the trick. It will fall off only if you are doing it wrongly.

Often a new trick is attempted and the skier comes nowhere near executing it. Don't despair, it could be a tiny thing going wrong which is exaggerated through the course of the trick. Just have a long hard think about it – using your brain is half the battle in trick skiing.

Never set a time limit for learning a trick, it is impossible to predict. For instance, I made a front to back two-ski step on the first attempt and then spent two months learning a toe-hold 360. Peter Bryant, whom I was training at the time as a dauphine, took more than a year over his front to back two-ski step but had the toe-hold 360 off pat in a week.

Three important points for beginners:

1 Don't worry about the amount of air you have under the skis when learning wake tricks. A wake trick is purely a surface trick performed in a different place. Getting daylight between your skis and the wake – as you must to perform the trick correctly – can come later.

2 Always finish a trick with both hands on the handle. There is bound to be slack rope in trick skiing – and with two hands you are more able

to correct bad landings. This is particularly important on wake tricks.

3 Keep both hands on the handle until a turn is properly under way. For some reason many beginners are inclined to start a trick *after* releasing one hand.

The following section contains a detailed description of the most commonly performed tricks. The order is deliberate: each trick builds on points from the previous one. New tricks are being added all the time, especially in championship skiing with its constant search for excellence. These more exotic tricks are not included – but all of them contain the basic manoeuvres detailed here:

Surface turns

Side slides

Type	*Description*	*Value*
Two-ski side slide	Turning both skis the same way at right angles to boat	20

How to do it   Keep skis between 2 and 4 in apart. Force them into the turn with a thrust of the hips keeping your body square with the skis but with your head still facing the boat. After starting the turns let go with the hand furthest from the boat, keeping the handle in and down with the other. Hold the right angle for a second or so and then return to normal skiing position, bringing the free hand back to the handle as you do so. The biggest hazard is the sudden decrease in drag which can send the skis sliding out. Counteract this by forcing the hips away from the boat and shoulders towards the boat. Feel your way into the trick by only turning half way at first and gradually increasing.

Type	*Description*	*Value*
One-ski side slide	Turning single ski at right angles to boat	70

How to do it   Same as above except that because the single ski will skid far more easily it is important to ensure that the back edge is down – again by leaning away from the boat slightly with your hips and towards the boat with your upper body.

Multiple turns

Type	*Description*	*Value*
Two-ski and one-ski 180 front to back and back to front	Continuation of side slide which follows through to the back skiing position	30 60

How to do them   These should be attempted only when you can do the side slide – except that now you lead into the turn with your head, as

Maria Victoria Carasco (Venezuela) world tricks champion doing a one-ski side slide

you will with all the following tricks. As you turn, reach behind yourself with your free hand ready to grab the handle as you complete the 180-degree turn. It is vital that you keep the other arm bent and resting virtually on the top of your buttocks. If it stretches away from the body your free hand has no chance of reaching the handle.

With the correct stance to begin with, your body will automatically lean away from the boat in a backward position, and this will counteract the unnatural pull. Keep the skis together otherwise the edge of the trailing ski will catch. Fix your eyes on the horizon all the way round. It is very important that when you have finished the trick and are in the back position that you hold it for practice, as I mentioned earlier.

On one ski extra care must be taken to perform the trick slowly and smoothly. With all the weight on one ski, balance is critical.

Type	Description	Value
Two-ski and	Continuation of 180	40
one-ski 360	until full circle	90
	is completed.	

How to do them Perform a normal 180 turn, pause in the back position and then continue to make the full turn. Repeat, returning in the opposite direction and pausing at the 180 mark. Keep doing these circles first one way then the other to prevent dizziness, and cut down on the half-way pause each time until the full circle is a continuous movement. Do them very slowly to start with, too much speed and effort will cost you control and balance, even when you are advanced too much speed will make you fall.

There is a possibility of rope slackness with these turns. Some skiers try to use it to their advantage by actually creating slack rope with a giant pull as they begin their turn. They are hoping to complete their turn before the line becomes taut again. It is an extremely bad manoeuvre, resulting in hasty ill-balanced turns and a poor finishing position. Always try to turn with a tight line.

Step overs

Type	Description	Value
Two-ski stepover	Literally stepping over	70
back to front	the rope with one foot so	
	that from skiing backwards	
	you turn to face the boat	
	again	

How to do it Get into position by performing a 180. Push the rope down below your backside, release one hand and place that through your legs and back onto the handle. Which hand that should be depends upon which ski you are going to step with. Left footed skiers should step with their right leg. If you step with the right hold with the right hand and vice versa. Therefore left hand goes round the side of left leg and right hand goes between legs. Both palms are up. You will find that your back will be bent because your arms are lower. Don't worry in this instance because it will also lower your centre of gravity. To ensure that your back is not too bent, keep your head up. Slowly put all your weight onto the foot you are going to ski on. Lift the other ski very gradually until the heel is tucked up and almost touching your buttocks. That way the back tip of the ski is above the tow-rope.

Many skiers find it a problem to step and turn at the same time. They are unsure how much effort to put into each manoeuvre and consequently either tackle the trick timidly or with too much zeal. Doing it my way, with the foot poised to cross the rope, you don't have to put any effort into the step, merely let the foot fall. All your energy can be concentrated into the turn. To do that let go of the handle outside the leg, place the suspended ski on the water, rotate the standing ski with a thrust from your hips and grab hold of the handle with both hands

58

again. You will probably sit down on the water the first time you attempt this trick and having both hands on the handle will give you more chance of righting yourself.

Also, the majority of falls with this trick are away from the boat and that is because skiers are putting their weight onto their heels. Keep the rope down and shoulders over the skis at all times.

Type	Description	Value
Two-ski stepover front to back	Same as above, except other way round	80

How to do it From experience, this is the toughest trick to learn up to now. But it shouldn't be. Skiers find it a totally unnatural movement and even some of the best have been stuck for months trying to master this trick. The main problem, again, is the two-in-one motion of

Karen Morse (GB) poised for a step from the back position

Heidi Richardson (GB) begins and completes a front to back step.

stepping and turning. True, there is a more definite stepping motion in this trick compared with the one above, but the same procedure of lifting the ski and holding it will halve the difficulties. Bring the knees up to the chest, resting the side of the ski against the rope.

Start to step with the ski before you begin to turn. The most common fault here is for people to throw their heads back, and then topple backwards. Counteract that by leaning forward with head and shoulders. As in the back-to-front step, let go of that hand as you make the step and then grab hold with two immediately you reach the backwards position. This cannot be a slow-motion turn because the ski will slip away. And, of course, keep the rope as low as possible without unbalancing yourself. The lower you have it the lower you need to step, the higher the more chance of unbalancing yourself.

Type	Description	Value
One-ski stepover back	Same as two-skis	110
to front and front to back		120

How to do it Principles are the same as for the previous two tricks. And as before, learn the back to front first. It's that much easier. Lower handle below buttocks. Take back foot out of binding, grasp handle through the legs with the correct hand (right foot step, right hand grasp) and turn very slowly. Stealth is essential because you have only one ski, and all your weight on it. It is difficult enough to stop in the final position without making matters worse by rushing. To be awarded the trick in competition you must let your free foot touch the water, not the spray to complete the trick.

Toe-holds

Type	Description	Value
Toe-hold side slide	Same as one-ski side slide, but in toe position	150

How to do it Put your foot in the toe-hold position and wait until you are totally balanced. Your toe-hold leg should be low with the knee well bent to act as the shock absorber, then as you turn you will automatically go into the correct 'comma' position, shoulders towards the boat, hips away. Push down with the back edge and turn slowly: too fast and you may not be able to stop. Hold for a split second only the first few times. There is some controversy whether you should go *up* into a toe-hold side slide or *down* into it. In other words, should you stand straight to start with and bend as you start the trick or vice versa. You will see champions using either method. Personally, I start off slightly bent and stay that way. Then there is no excess body movement.

Type	Description	Value
Reverse toe-hold side slide	Same as above but turning other way	230

How to do it This is harder than the ordinary toe-hold side slide

△ *Maria Esperanza Carasco (Venezuela) using the arm to maintain balance*

Easy for some . . . the author makes the tricky toe-hold side slide seem so simple △

because your body is turning through the leg holding the tow-rope. Start with the leg holding the handle extended in front of you. Pull in with the leg by bending the knee before you start the turn. You must not lift the leg to pull, that will throw your upper body backwards. But you must raise the leg as you turn so that at the end of the turn you can take the pull as high as possible towards the centre of the body. If you take it low down, around calf level, the ski will be yanked out. As you turn, rest the ankle of the pulling leg on, or just above the knee of your standing leg and be sure your weight is forward in the comma position, keeping the back edge of the ski down. The pull is off-centre so it will automatically return you to the front.

Type	Description	Value
Toe-hold 180 front to back	Half a circle with toe-hold grip	100

How to do it The toe-hold leg should be bent and in towards the body a little. Your weight must be kept over the ski at all times, so when you

Maria Esperanza Carasco (Venezuela) executes a perfect toe-hold side slide

turn and have your back to the boat, arch shoulders. Some instructors believe that you should give a little hop to relieve pressure at the start of the turn. I disagree. It is impossible to hop in the middle of other toe-holds so if you learn the 180 without you are more prepared for those advanced tricks. If you feel yourself falling away from the boat in the back position you can push your hands into the water and use them as extra skis to recover. (See Fig.13.)

Type	Description	Value
Toe-hold 180 back to front	As above, but starting with back to boat	120

How to do it   A common fault is that skiers fail to get their weight far enough forward as they turn to the front. Reach forward as you turn as if you were taking hold of the handle and that will help you maintain the correct balance.

Type	Description	Value
Reverse toe-hold 180 front to back and back to front	Opposite way round to normal 180	110 130

How to do them   With difficulty. Same principles as for the reverse toe-hold side slide. Pull before you turn, it is hard to do both at once without falling. As you turn lift the pulling leg and rest the outside of that ankle against, or just above the knee of the standing leg. Arch your back towards the boat. The pull is off centre so it will automatically bring you back round again, once the impetus from your turn is spent. As you come towards the front, round your shoulders and reach out as if to take the handle. That will bring your weight forward. (See Fig.14.)

Type	Description	Value
Toe-hold 360	Complete circle in toe-hold position	220

How to do it Wrap toe-hold leg behind standing leg with the ankle wedged into the knee. Hook your foot into the toe-hold and swivel the toe-hold downwards so that it is resting in its natural position across the top of your foot. (Some people allow the action of the trick itself to turn their foot into the toe-hold, but I always found my way much more comfortable.) Hold onto the rope with both hands about 12 in in front of your foot but do not pull up on the rope, that will only cause slack when you let go to start the turn. If you don't hold on with your hands you will spin out with the pull too soon. If your toe-rope leg is wedged in the correct position you will not have to bend the body too much to take hold of the rope. Release your hands, wait for the pull and allow the boat to spin you round slowly. Keep the shoulders square with the ski. Keep the arms down, lifting them will unsettle the upper body; but use them to balance. For learning purposes stop in the backward position. It is too much to expect to get all the way round on the first couple of attempts. Your back should be arched towards the boat in the back position. From there you continue round as in the normal 180 back to front toe-hold. Throughout the trick, ensure the knees remain bent and the body down.

Type	Description	Value
Reverse toe-hold 360	Same as above turning other way	300

How to do it It is literally a backwards replay of the trick above. You start with your leg extended and end wrapped around your standing knee, in exactly the same way as you begin the normal toe-hold 360. It is a difficult trick and skiers tend to turn very fast to get it over with. Consequently, by the time they are coming into the forward position they are all over the place. You will need, however, to pull hard to get the sufficient momentum to send you into the turn.

Type	Description	Value
Toe-hold 360	As above but starting	250
Back to back and reverse	with back to boat	280

How to do them First use a toe-hold reverse 180 to get in position with your back to the boat. Both tricks are combinations of the two toe-hold 180s without a pause in the middle. They are always performed one after the other because if they are executed independently in a competition the rules state that the second one will not be counted. The back to back coming out of the 180 reverse position should be relatively easy providing that during the first half of the trick the toe-hold leg is kept tucked in to provide a powerful fluid pull, for the second half. The back to back coming out of the normal 180 position is more difficult because you must pull and turn simultaneously during the first 180. The faster you do it the harder it is. Learn with a pause in between the two 180s.

Type	Description	Value
Toe-hold 540	*Half a turn more*	*400*
front to back	than the 360	

How to do it Start in the toe-hold 360 wrapped position, spin out and do the 180 toe reverse. It is essential to have absolute control when you first come to the front position. Let the toe-hold foot out slightly more than normal so that you can pull it in as you do the second part of the toe 360 and go into the reverse 180 without the slightest pause. Again learn with a pause, this time at the front.

Figure 13

Figure 14

Type	Description	Value
Toe-hold back to front 540	Same as above, starting with back to boat	400

How to do it Start in the toe 180 backward reverse position. Spin out of that, holding your leg in powerfully to maintain the impetus for the toe-hold reverse 360 which follows.

Wake turns

Multiple turns

Type	Description	Value
Two-ski and one-ski 180 front to back and back to front	Half a circle off the wake	50

How to do them Same as the surface 180s, only coming off the top of the wake. At first it doesn't matter if there is no air at all between your skis and the water, that will come. Let the wake do the work for you. There is no need to throw an enormous amount of effort into it; the best wake tricks are performed with ease. Learn the front to back going from inside to outside the wake and the back to front from outside to inside. With the back to front it all has to be done by feel because you can't see the wake coming.

A lot of learners are so anxious to find the wake that they begin their turn immediately they reach it, instead of waiting for the peak.

Type	Description	Value
Two-ski and one-ski 360 (helicopter)	Full circle off the wake	110 150

How to do them The difficulty with this trick is gaining sufficient time in the air to complete all the handle work necessary for a 360 degree turn. For learning purposes one way out is to wrap the rope around the body before you start. Practise this by wrapping and spin-ning on the surface directly behind the boat. This is the first instance where learning the trick coming into the wake helps.

Wrap the rope around your side, at hip level to keep the pull in the correct place, grab the handle behind your back with the palm of the hand away from the body. The little finger should be next to the edge of the handle behind you. The other hand should grasp the rope in front to steady you against the uncentralised pull. Do not wrap the rope more than half way round your body. You are shortening the rope by wrapping, and the shorter it gets the more slack you have to deal with as you release it to begin the spin. Let go of the rope in front of you as you reach the top of the wake. That will allow the sideways pull to spin you out of the wrap. You do nothing. Just keep your knees bent, head up, back straight. Concentrate on keeping the handle arm close to the body as you turn, and be ready to grab hold with the other hand as you hit the front, before the full force of the pull comes back.

Type	Description	Value
One-ski 360 back to back and reverse	Turning full circle off wake starting with back to boat	210

How to do them Get into position with a 180 turn, but instead of turning everything round merely turn the ski and keep the rest of your body pointing forwards as far as possible. Bring the handle in to your hip and exaggerate the bend of the knees. It is an extremely hard position to hold, and you will probably not succeed for the first few attempts. The slower you turn into the position in the first place, the less likely you are to be pulled out of it. In fact, the position you settle in will be about 170 degrees instead of 180 as you traverse.

If you are going to perform a position, turn to the left and a spin out to the right, you will start by going into the right hand wake. Ski to the wake in the back position and try to feel the top of the wake. It is the first time you have approached the wake backwards from the inside, and it is a strange feeling. Do a 180 back to front. This will carry you outside the wake. Return to the middle, then ski into the same wake again and perform a front to back 180. These are the two halves of the trick. Repeat them separately until you are totally familiarized – then join them together. Now is the time to learn the reverse back to back coming into the wake from the outside using the same stage-by-stage procedure. Coming out of the second back to back you can land one-handed, which allows the boat to pull you round to the front.

Type	Description	Value
One-ski 540 front to back	One and a half turns coming off wake, starting with front to boat	310

How to do it This can either be performed by wrapping, or hand to hand. It is a combination of a front to front 360 followed by a 180 and should be learnt with a slight pause in between these two tricks. Because you need a lot of spin you must not waste effort jumping, the wake will take care of that. Keep the spin smooth, don't throw yourself into it. On landing come immediately to the front position to steady yourself. Learn both the normal and reverse coming into the wake, it's easier that way. In competition you can put them together on any wake.

Type	Description	Value
One-ski 540 back to front	One and a half turns coming off wake starting with back to boat	320

How to do it Do the 180 position turn in the same way as you do the 360 back to back. Go from outside to inside the wake. Hit the top of the wake and spin out. The backwards position turn will feel more comfortable one way round, of course. For instance, if you are a left foot forward skier you can face towards the boat far more easily when you are turned to the left. Timing is critical with the reverse because turning is that much more difficult when you are coming into the wake backwards in that position. A pause in the back position after the first 360 can be helpful in the learning process.

The author demonstrates the wake 360 wrap

Stepovers

Type	Description	Value
Two-ski and one-ski stepover back to front and front to back	Stepping over tow-rope on the wake and turning half circle	110

How to do it   Same as the surface step except that you use the wake to get height off the water. Important to judge your speed into the wake correctly to maintain good balance. As you become more advanced in step turns you will have the strength and expertise to use only one hand on the handle during a step sequence, keeping the other free for balancing. On one ski it is imperative to cut slowly to the wake.

Type	Description	Value
One-ski stepover 360 and reverse	Stepping over the tow-rope on the wake and ending with front to boat	260

How to do them   The normal trick is performed hand to hand; the reverse is wrapped. Both are learnt going from outside the wake. In the normal version the step is carried out during the first 180. The main problem is staying over the ski, so the weight must be on the front of the foot, without allowing the shoulders to come too far forwards. That is a difficult position to spin from and in attempting to do so a lot of skiers throw their heads and shoulders back.

It is easier to start in the standard position and then shift your weight forward by bringing the shoulders over the arms as you start the turn. Keep the standing leg and stepping leg bent all the time. Start to raise the leg and lead with it into the turn during the final phase of your approach to the wake so that the leg is almost over the

The author in a 180 wrapped position turn.

Maria Victoria Carasco (Venezuela) in the middle of a wake 180 back to front △

line by the time you have reached the top of the wake. Don't worry about getting height off the wake the first few times, just feel the trick.

In the reverse, the step comes in the second 180 of the turn. Wrap with your arm through your leg (left arm for right foot skiers and vice versa) and round back of the skiing leg. The rope comes round the outside of the skiing leg. Wrap as high as possible up the leg because that will enable you to keep your upper body reasonably straight ready for the spin to come. The stepping leg must be kept level with the skiing leg and not dragging behind in the water, that will pull your body off square.

Hold the rope in front with your other hand, then as you release that the off-central pull of the boat will take you into the spin and step. Because the pull is relatively low down your body, the tendency is to fall backwards. So double check you have the weight on the balls of your feet.

69

Type	Description	Value
One-ski stepover 360 back to back and reverse	Stepping over tow-rope on the wake and turning full circle, starting and ending with back to boat	260

How to do them Difficult tricks because you have to land backwards with one foot on the ski after considerable spin. The secret is to put in as little effort as possible. These require nowhere near the momentum of a front to front. Start in the backward step position, with the rope between your legs. In the normal turn begin your turn as you come into the wake so that the leg is almost above the rope at the top of the wake. Keep your upper body as straight as possible and both knees bent, that will keep the spin vertical and make landing easier. The step will bring you into the normal forward skiing position in the air. Pass the handle and execute a final 180. Keep the towing arm in at all times. If it is out with this trick when you land you have little chance of remaining upright. Immediately you land return to the front position as this will have a steadying effect.

To perform the reverse, start in the normal backwards skiing position holding the rope with both hands in the pit of your back. On the

Liz Allen Shetter, triple world champion, is technically faultless as she executes a wake 360 on one ski

top of the wake do a back to back turn. Keep the arms low because in the second part of the turn you are going to step and then land in that stepped position with the rope between your legs.

Toe-holds

Type	*Description*	*Value*
Toe-hold 180 front to	Half a circle off the wake	150
back and back to front	in a toe-hold position	180

How to do them The front to back is learnt going from inside to outside the wake. The back to front from outside to inside the wake. For the front to back, start in the normal toe-hold skiing position with your shoulders over the ski. Turn at the top of the wake, and as you do so, arch your back to keep your weight central on the ski. For the more difficult back to front, you must stand straight on the ski with the back arched towards the boat on approach. Then as you turn and land the tendency to fall away will be counteracted. Also, as you land, bring your head and shoulders forward as if you were reaching for the handle.

Type	*Description*	*Value*
Toe-hold 360	Full circle in toe-hold	300
	position starting and ending	
	with front to boat	

How to do it Same wrap as the toe-hold 360, high behind the knee so your body remains as vertical as possible. Not too much speed off the top of the wake, just sufficient to carry you round. Keep pulling leg bent and in, there will always be a snap in the rope in this trick because there is scarcely anything to pull against whilst you are in the air. The knees must be bent to absorb the sudden pull. Don't attempt to jump off the wake, that is the surest way to disaster in this trick, more than any other. As you land have a good bend in the skiing leg and reach forward with your head and shoulders to keep the weight over the ski and be prepared for a final snap on the rope. Lean from outside to inside.

Type	*Description*	*Value*
Toe-hold 360	As above, starting and	330
back to back	ending with back to boat	

How to do it If you have learnt the toe-hold 360 surface back to back correctly this should present no great hazards. If you are left foot forward, go outside the right hand wake and vice versa. At the very last second as you come into the top of the wake do a toe reverse. Try and hold it until the pull returns and then do a normal 360 back to back in the air. Keep the shoulders arched towards the boat in the back position. Land as upright as possible because then you are ready to go on to the next trick sequence. This should be relatively easy to do as you are landing in the toe-hold back position, which is a simple stance to recover from, and a powerful skiing position.

△ *The author begins a perfect wake step front to back*

The same trick from a different angle △

Rick McCormick (USA), world champion, shows similar style

Chantal Escot (France) performing a wake step back to front on one ski. Note the fine position of the handle – down and in – and her free hand ready to grasp the handle

Maria Victoria Carasco (Venezuela) wrapping for a wake 360 step

The author performing a toe-hold wake 180 front to back

Maria Victoria Carasco (Venezuela) performing the toe-hold wake 180 back to front

Carlos Suarez (Venezuela), world champion, in the middle of a toe-hold wake sequence

Skiing, even at the top level, should be fun, and here the author enjoys himself

Putting a run together

This, obviously, becomes harder the more tricks you learn. A trick run is not a chain of individual tricks, but an organised sequence which flows and eliminates time wastage.

In competition skiing you are given two runs of twenty seconds each to perform your repertoire and for the majority of skiers that means more time than tricks. But, as far as I am concerned, one side slide is sufficient to enter a tournament. You can do your side slide, attempt a 180 and fall. Nobody will realise you cannot do any other tricks and you will have gained invaluable experience.

Remember that great world champion Liz Allen scored precisely 110 trick points during the world championships in Bogota. If the best can perform like that, what's stopping you having a go? But even if you have only a handful of tricks, it is essential you put them in the right order – and that means a rhythmic, comfortable sequence. That sounds so logical as to be not worth saying, yet dozens of potentially fine trick skiers thwart themselves by attempting high-value tricks in a disjointed sequence in the bid to score heavily.

On the other hand, a particularly difficult trick may fit very well at the start of your run. But if you are likely to fall you should discard it. It is far better to get some points in the bank with a succession of easier, less valuable tricks. For instance, a toe-wake 360 is a high scoring trick but to perform it effectively the chances are you have to include it at the start of the run so you can use the approach to get in position. It is a trick I do fairly well but I refuse to risk it unless I am desperate for points. In European competition I used it about once every five runs.

I also feel it is wrong suddenly to add a high-scoring but unsure trick at the end of the run. Of course it does no harm if you fall on it, the run is over anyway. What does do the damage is the diversion it causes to your concentration. For, no matter how hard you try to shut your mind during a run you will always be conscious of the fact that a difficult trick is coming up. That distraction is fatal.

Concentration is everything. It is staggering the number of world-class skiers I have seen fall on a one-ski 360. That is simply because the trick is easy enough to lull them into a false security. Be aware all the time of the trick you are performing; no matter how simple it is, it is even easier to fall.

Aim for consistency, too. Develop a trick run and stick with it throughout a season instead of constantly chopping and changing. And start the first run with a series of easy tricks. The confidence these give you plus the familiarity will allow you to settle down and pace yourself in competition, ease the pressure, and give you that bit more time to judge the particular conditions of the course.

There will come a point for the progressive skier where he has to jettison certain tricks in favour of higher value ones. This is a galling experience as he has probably spent many hours perfecting the trick he is now about to toss aside. He should console himself in the knowledge that each trick learnt creates a foundation for the more advanced ones. Knowledge is never wasted in trick skiing.

Avoid hurrying during a competition run. Doing tricks slowly gives you a greater margin of error and is usually quicker in the long run because you will need less time to steady yourself between each trick. The more haste, the more likelihood of a fall. If you find you are spending excessive time between wake tricks you should shorten the rope to bring yourself as close to the wake as possible without hindering control. And beware of jumping too high off the wake; that costs time as well.

As you grow more and more familiar with a run, so you will be able to speed up a little and add another trick or two. But this modification must be a gradual affair. Human nature always makes us want to do better than our best. The clever skier realises this is not possible.

Use your common sense when deciding which tricks to use. For instance, if two side slides, worth 140 points, take you two seconds and a helicopter, worth 150 points, takes three seconds, the side slides are better value.

Clarity is vital with every trick. Give them a lot of definition and expression otherwise, if there is a reasonable doubt, the judges will mark you down. This is particularly important in rough water where the wave patterns will obscure timid tricks.

Finally, there is no short cut to trick skiing success – it is earned through hours of hard work and practice. But don't overdo it, that merely leads to strains and frustrating time off the water. Ten to fifteen minutes of concentrated effort will be far better than longer sessions where both the skier and the boat driver lose their edge.

Always attempt new tricks. Practising the same ones day after day may be reassuring but it is no way to progress. Don't be too fussy about water conditions – the most successful skiers are those who can operate whatever the weather. And if a trick gives you a lot of trouble, don't just toss it away. Take time off from it, analyse and come back to it. It will seem a whole lot different after a break.

4 Jumping

Jumping is the easiest part of waterskiing to learn, the most thrilling – and perfectly safe in the early stages.

Forget all those stories about horrendous injuries and people flying off the ramp in all directions and at all degrees. Most of them are exaggerated.

Jumping injuries invariably happen only at competition level when skiers are straining for extra speed and height. At these times, moving at more than 60 mph (100 kmph) and leaping more than 160 ft (50 m) it is certainly dangerous. But to start with you can count yourself unlucky if you collect a bruise, pulled muscle or graze.

The ramp

A sturdy, two-platform construction of wood or metal, 24 ft (7 m) long and 14 ft (4 m) wide. Wooden ramps feel better to skiers because they are that much softer, but metal ramps produce longer jumps. Both have a top platform of plywood coated with wax or fibreglass.

The ramp is anchored to the bottom by four weighted guy ropes – the two at the lowered end angle straight down, the two at the blunt end cross to provide greater stability. Somewhat confusingly, this blunt end is usually referred to as the 'front' of the ramp.

The ramp floats on styrofoam or empty steel drums. The height is adjusted by a powerful hydraulic jack at the blunt end.

The top right edge should be smooth because the rope runs along there as the skier jumps, but the rest should allow a modicum of traction. If it is too smooth, it will have a suction effect on the skis like glass rubbing on glass. The ideal ramp will have the same speed as the surface of the water.

More sophisticated ramps have water sprinklers, but a splash down with a bucket before each jump will do just as well.

Safety is the priority in jumping, so watch these five points:

1 The bottom lip of the ramp must be at least 1 ft under the water to prevent ski fins catching on take-off.
2 Regular checks must be made for screws worked loose by the constant pounding.
3 The ramp should be painted a medium, neutral colour. White dazzles and makes it appear nearer; black bodes evil and sits back.
4 Triangles of wood or fibreglass along the side of the ramp – called

'side curtains' – must be fitted as you advance. These are angled to the water and will deflect your skis if you misjudge your approach as is possible at the higher speeds.

5 Ensure that any bow in the surface is upwards. Downwards bow will tip the skier forwards. Ideally, the surface should be totally flat.

Height of ramp

In Britain, men's competition height is 6 ft (1·80 m), junior boys 5 ft 6 in (1·65 m) and everyone else 5 ft (1·50 m). In America only expert men are allowed over 6 ft (1·80 m). Men jump at 5 ft 6 in (1·65 m), the rest at 5 ft (1·50 m).

Skis

Normal skis can be worn, but to avoid breakage and expense I strongly advise using the specially constructed heavy-duty jumpers. Surprisingly jump skis do have fins – without them you would slide around on the water. Jump skis need care and maintenance to keep the bottoms smooth otherwise you will generate drag on the water and the ramp. Check your skis for rough edges after every session; no matter how smooth the ramp, the skis will wear. Some skiers sensibly cover all fastening nuts and bolts with protective tape so they do not cut if the ski comes off. Finally, ensure bindings are firm but not so tight as to prevent your feet popping out in the event of a fall.

Clothing

Life jackets must be worn, both for flotation and protection. It is highly unlikely that you will knock yourself out while jumping, but it is possible. More likely, you will take a few heavy falls and the jacket will protect your ribs. Make sure it fits snugly. The force of hitting the water could pull it off.

Crash helmets also should be worn, especially as you progress. You will see champions jumping without. They need their heads examined as well as protected. Flying skis do not discriminate.

I recommend wearing a short wet suit. Failing that a pair of cut-offs in heavy fabric such as denim. The impact of landing creates jets of water and these will shoot painfully up your legs and into your body unless you wear something tight and tough around your thighs.

Beginners

Jumping is not recommended for absolute beginners. You should at least have the confidence of competent mono-skiing before setting your sights on the ramp. The more experience you have, the less likely you are to frighten yourself on your first jump. Do not go straight from mono-skiing to jumping; get the feel of two skis again.

Do not practise by jumping the wake. This is a controversial issue and worth examining thoroughly. Jumping the wake does have advantages, but I believe they are far outweighed by the disadvantages.

Advantages: It gives you the feel of going through the air and of landing.

Disadvantages: (a) To get off the water you must spring and when you come to the ramp as a beginner this is just what you do not want. (b) Springing off the wake engenders a lot of body movement. Your head and shoulders go back and your arms come up. Again this is precisely what you do not want when you come to the ramp.

Once learnt these bad habits are extremely difficult to shake off and will seriously retard the novice jumper.

Jumping should not be encouraged for children under thirteen. Their backs are not sufficiently formed to take the strains incurred. Tell them to perfect their trick skiing instead. There is plenty of time and it will be far quicker and easier to learn jumping when they have the necessary power.

Everyone is frightened the first time, that's natural. The ramp looks like the side of a house as you set off, but it is amazing the number of skiers who return after their first taste with a 'Shucks, there's nothing to it' reaction. If it's any comfort, I have never seen anybody hurt themselves with their first jump – even when they have fallen headlong.

The ramp should be set as low as it will go for the first jump. Most reduce to 5 ft (1·50 m), some to as low as 3 ft (1 m). Remember, the angle is nowhere near as acute as it looks. At 4 ft the ramp slopes at just 10½ degrees.

Stance

This stance applies throughout jumping – from novice to expert:

Figure 15

1 Skis 8–10 in (20–25 cm) apart.

2 Knees bent in relaxed but powerful position. (Cocked, in fact, like a spring ready to explode open.)

3 Slight forward bend in the waist so the shoulders are over the knees and feet in such a way that a plumb line would touch all three points. (If you stand too bent you are likely to fold up with the impact of the ramp; too upright and you could be thrown backwards.)

4 Weight on the balls of the feet. (Essential for a two-point landing.)

5 Head up with eyes looking at horizon. (You will look down to judge landings when you have advanced, but looking down as a beginner automatically makes you flinch your body away from the water.)

6 Elbows directly in line with your sides and pressed in against the life jacket. (If your arms are out as you come to the ramp you have no chance.)

7 Forearms sloping at 45 degrees down to the handle, keeping the handle a few inches away from the hips. (This ensures the pull is taken at the hips.)

Grip

Right palm down, left palm up. The boat *always* passes to the right of the ramp and this grip is the most comfortable for taking the pull from that direction.

Land practice

Simulate your stance only, wearing all the necessary equipment. Do not attempt to jump as it will be nothing like the real thing and only give you false impressions. Also, for the first few attempts you will not try to spring anyway as I shall explain.

The first approach

The skier uses the full 75 ft (23 m) rope (as does the expert) and approaches the ramp with a long run in to make sure he is completely settled. The boat should be running 10–15 ft (3–5 m) away from the right edge of the ramp. Any closer and the skier is likely to land on or very near to the wake and he has enough on his mind at the moment without that. The boat speed should be between 18–22 mph (30–37 kmph) depending on weight. Sufficient for him to be plopped over the ramp and not so fast that he is thrown up by it.

Stand outside the left-hand wake, set your stance, then pull out to the left of the boat and line yourself up with the bottom left edge of the ramp. As you are running parallel to the boat and just behind it you will be pulling on your left edge. About 10 ft (3 m) from the ramp flatten off the skis – this will have the effect of making the skis' path up the ramp slightly diagonal from left to right because you will be pulled directly towards the boat. This will bring your point of impact with the ramp to somewhere between left edge and centre. It is important to get this line right.

If you attempt to go straight up the middle of the ramp your skis will still be on edge, pulling away from the boat, and will slide out from under you. Later on you will be edging all the way to the ramp, but at this stage you don't have the expertise to handle it.

As you flatten off the skis aim yourself for the pylon in the boat as if you wanted to land on top of it. And then *freeze*.

Do absolutely nothing for those last 10 ft or when you hit the ramp. Blink if you must, but that's all. Just let the boat pull you over the ramp

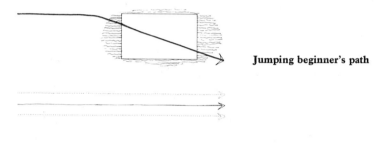

Jumping beginner's path

14 m

and plop you down on the other side. As you land give slightly in the knees, allow yourself to be towed away and then – unfreeze.

You will want to move because it is a strange experience and you are bound to feel a little unsteady. You must resist all temptation and hold your position.

The tilt of the ramp will tend to throw you back so it is vital you keep your weight well forward. That takes a bit of nerve.

And keep your arms down at hip level. If you are thrown backwards the great tendency is to pull yourself into position. That forces the arms up and will put you into even worse trouble.

Remember to keep your eyes fixed on the horizon. Looking down at all that water rushing up to meet you will only make you recoil at this elementary stage.

The most common mistake on landing is to sit back on the skis. This is because people do not have the nerve to get themselves forwards enough and it is more a sign of success to fall over the skis.

Don't be fooled if you are pulled forwards into the water *after* sitting back on your skis. I have known a lot of people go backwards, get an almighty tug which pitches them headlong, and then complain that it happened because they were too far forward.

If your skis splay on the ramp they are too far apart. If your vertical balance is unsteady they are too close together.

Frans Oberleitner (Austria) hangs on with hope and a prayer

Maria Victoria Carasco (Venezuela) is in all kinds of trouble, but still holding onto the rope

Rick McCormick (USA) in trouble, but still relaxed and confident of recovery

Falls

There is one golden rule about falls which applies especially to more advanced jumpers, but also to beginners: hold on to the handle at all costs. Once you have decided to take the jump and are on the ramp you are committed. Whatever shape you get into from then on – upside down, skis splayed – does not matter. You hang on until you hit the water.

There are two reasons why:

1 In advanced skiing it is your only hope of righting yourself. I have been upside down and righted myself by holding on to the handle.

2 It can drag you clear of flying skis if you fall. I'm not saying you will never be hit by skis, but it will reduce considerably the likelihood.

Intermediate

When you have managed to land on your feet a few times you can start making it more difficult. Raise the ramp to 5 ft (1·50 m) and gradually raise the speed of the boat to about 30 mph (48 kmph). There is no point in going any faster as that is the maximum speed for a 5 ft (1·50 m) ramp and the most comfortable to learn at.

You will have noticed a large buoy to the right-hand side of the ramp and some 45 ft (14 m) away from the centre of the ramp. This is the '14-metre buoy' and now is the time to start making use of it. It is there to mark a standard distance that the boat should travel wide of the ramp. So, again in gradual stages, start pushing the boat wider of the ramp until it is just inside that buoy.

Meanwhile, you continue in the same position as before except that now you start flattening off the skis a little later and aim more for the middle of the ramp. The increased speed will counteract the angle of the boat and you will be pulled off the top slightly right of centre.

Be prepared for the increasingly strong impact with the ramp – and the fact that you will now be jumping around 40 ft (12 m) compared to the 10–15 you started with.

Soon after you begin the intermediate stage of increasing the speed and angle you should also start tackling the spring.

The impact shows on the face of Mike Suyderhoud (USA) as he hits the ramp

Spring

This is another jumping milestone which people seem to feel they have to write their last will and testament before attempting. In truth, the spring is so simple it is laughable. All you do is unbend your legs as you hit the ramp. You do *not* try to jump as that merely has the effect of unsettling your arms and shoulders which will probably throw you backwards and reduce the distance you jump.

At first, the straightening of the knees should be a slowish, almost hesitant, movement, gradually speeded up until it becomes an explosive little pop. In fact, 'pop' for me is so absolutely descriptive of the action that I never refer to it by any other word. Trying an almighty spring is impossible at higher speeds – as well as unbalancing – so you might just as well start the way you mean to go on with a short, sharp pop.

The pop is controlled entirely by the knees. If your knees are too bent you will have less power; if they are too straight you will have less potential power. As you uncoil them you should push directly down (Fig. 16) against the ramp with the weight on the balls of your feet. Do not aim to pop the body forward (Fig. 17) as this will at best give you a low trajectory and at worst send you tumbling over the front of the skis. You have the speed, all you need is height and this is most effectively gained by springing directly upwards. The boat will do the rest.

Where you pop depends upon the speed of the boat. For the first few times you should start the movement in the middle of the ramp because by the time you have straightened up you will be perfectly placed on the top. As your reflexes quicken you will have to leave it later to catch the very top of the ramp.

If you hit the ramp in the correct skiing position and time the pop correctly, it feels effortless – like the perfectly-timed golf or cricket stroke.

Of course, as you progress and reach speeds of 60 mph (100 kmph) and upwards the pop has to be instantaneous with hitting the ramp. At 70 mph (115 kmph) you are on the ramp for about one-fifth of a second. I have even seen photographs where skiers are starting to pop before they have reached the ramp.

Even the best mistime their pop under these circumstances and are airborne before they have uncoiled. I remember America's Wayne Grimditch failed to time one pop correctly at Thorpe Water Park, Surrey, in 1975 – yet he still won the world jump title. Obviously, then, a good pop is not essential. But I wonder how much further Grimditch might have jumped had he got it right?

I have jumped more than 160 ft (50 m) while missing out my pop completely. But when I scored a world record 176 ft 6½ in (53·80 m) I put both pop and acceleration into the ramp together correctly. This acceleration, known as 'cutting', should always be considered far more important than popping – as I will explain later.

Figure 16

Figure 17

There are three other terms you will often come across in jumping:

Crush   The opposite to spring and means, as its name implies, when your upper body or legs collapse with the impact of the ramp.

Jam   Halfway between spring and crush. In other words, bracing yourself as you hit the ramp and freezing.

Spread   The splay which results from hitting the ramp with your skis too far apart.

Single cut path

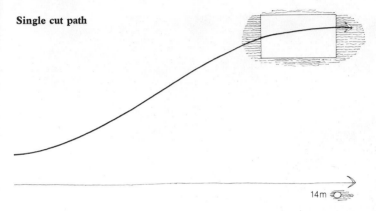

Cutting

This is a precise science and the most important aspect of jumping; without a well-judged cut you will never gain distance. The narrower the angle of your cut, the more speed you have into the ramp.

You are ready to start cutting once you have perfected the pop with the boat travelling about 30 mph (48 kmph) and just inside the 45-ft (14-m) buoy. For your first few attempts at cutting you should forget all about popping and concentrate purely on getting used to the different angle of approach.

Ski just outside the left-hand wake. Don't start off inside the wake; it is an obstacle which has to be negotiated and there is no point making affairs more difficult than they are.

Try a fairly gradual cut the first time and aim to hit the *middle* of the ramp. This gives you a margin of error either way which will be vital when you reach the greater speeds and sharper cuts.

Many people think the perfect place to enter the jump at speed is the right-hand bottom. But you need only an error of inches to be sent crashing into the side curtains. That could be caused by the boat driver or even a change in conditions. So play it safe and go into the middle. With the sharpest possible cut, you use only half the ramp, so why not use the safer half?

Start the cut with a smooth, controlled turn and then maintain a

87

powerful progressive angle up to – and even over – the ramp. Keep your whole body – knees, hips, shoulders and head – square to the direction in which you are travelling. Never open your body to the boat.

The whole point of cutting is that you should be at maximum speed when you hit the ramp. So you must now stop gliding onto it and start edging through. It is easier than it sounds because of the greater angle and higher speed, but I admit it does require a bit of nerve. Even good-class skiers are prone to 'chicken out' several yards from the ramp and coast through. Another general fear is that they are going to slide out on the ramp because they are leaning against the boat. In fact, it is

Bruce Cockburn (Australia) shows you can hit the ramp on the lean without disaster

precisely this lean and pull away from the boat which keeps the skier well balanced. One counteracts the other. The harder you edge and lean the more powerfully the boat will pull. Aim for a modest angle the first time, little will be gained by going hellbent at the ramp at this stage no matter how brave you are.

As you approach the ramp the change in angle of the pull from the boat will automatically straighten you out of your lean a little. Hold the pull down at your hip. There should be no slack rope at any time. If there is you have not edged all the way.

Hardly anybody gets his cut right at the first attempt. Several sessions should be spent perfecting it as it forms the basis of good jumping. Don't push yourself too quickly – in jumping you should always stay inside your limits.

Add the pop and gradually cut later and later. The object is not so much to increase the speed at this stage as to familiarise yourself with the angle of approach. The narrower the angle, the more acceleration you will be able to develop as you advance.

Move inside the wake and learn to cut through that as well – and then finally push the boat just outside the 45-ft (14-m) buoy for what is recognised as the perfect jumping position.

Some common faults to avoid

1 Do not rock back on your heels in an effort to obtain more speed. This will, in fact, make you go faster through the water with less effort but it will also lessen the bite of the skis. That will widen your angle of approach and, apart from causing misjudgements, rob you of impetus into the ramp.

Max Hofer (Italy) didn't keep his arms in

Also, you will be leaning back when you hit the ramp and your skis could slide out in front of you. Keep the weight forward through the balls of the feet with your shoulders over the skis at all times.
2 Don't allow the arms to be pulled straight. This is very easy to do at these speeds because the pull is increasing all the way into the ramp. Keep your arms in and down otherwise you will lose power and could be pulled forwards over your skis.
3 Don't allow your landings to become sloppy. Some skiers seem to think that they can start sitting back on their skis once they have mastered the techniques of cutting and popping. Good two-point landings become increasingly essential to powerful, controlled jumping as you land wider and wider of the boat. If you land too far back on your skis there is insufficient forwards pull to bring you back up again.
4 Do not become reliant on landmarks for gauging the start of a cut. They will not be there when you move to a different course.

Mike Suyderhoud (USA) lands ungracefully

Wayne Grimditch, US world champion, with his weight over the skis, explodes into the water on landing

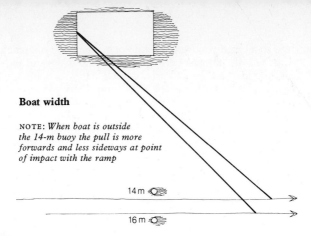

Boat width

NOTE: *When boat is outside the 14-m buoy the pull is more forwards and less sideways at point of impact with the ramp*

14 m

16 m

Position of boat

The 14-metre buoy is considered by most expert jumpers to be the optimum position for the boat because the pull increases steadily and helps you all the way to the ramp. If the boat is further out, the pull eases before you reach the ramp. Further inside the buoy and you have insufficient time between the wake and the ramp to accelerate effectively.

It was fashionable at one time to push the boat 60 ft (18 m) out and take a mighty swing at the ramp. But the sideways pull was so colossal that the skier banked alarmingly in the air, losing distance.

Refusals

Just as it is essential that you hold onto the handle whatever happens once you are on the ramp, it is equally important to know when and

Not this time . . . Liz Allen Shetter, triple world champion, refuses a jump and skis safely past the far side of the ramp

how to let go if you want to refuse a jump before you reach the ramp. That failsafe point is between the second wake and the ramp.

If you feel you are too early or too late in your approach let go of the handle and swerve to the left of the ramp. Once you have slowed down and passed the ramp swerve to the right ready for the boat to pick you up. On no account refuse by keeping the handle, attempting to change edges and cutting to the right-hand side of the ramp. At these sort of speeds your power to change direction is minimal and if you try you will probably lose control and could even crash headlong into the ramp.

You can refuse a jump up to the final split second before reaching the ramp. A really late refusal will end with you skimming over the left corner of the ramp – but that is far preferable to accepting the jump and compounding the error on the ramp.

Some skiers dislike refusing, believing they are wasting a ski or being timid. One side-effect is that they constantly cut very gently to prevent a refusal and never experiment to see how late they could leave it. When I was learning to double cut I refused four out of five jumps – and even five out of five.

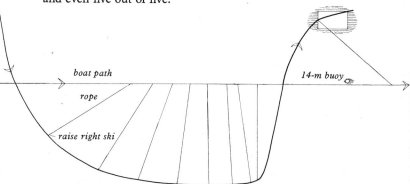

Advanced approach showing rope position at various points

Double cut

When you have mastered the single cut you are ready to try the double cut across both wakes which gives far more angle and, therefore, far more speed into the ramp. For this you must get as wide of the right-hand side of the boat as possible. Then turn your skis towards the wake and accelerate smoothly and powerfully through and onto the ramp. Try this modestly and without pop for the first few times.

As you become more expert you will be able to pull wider and wider of the boat before starting your cut. Lifting the right ski will gain you more width because the sudden reduction in drag will send you shooting out. But despite all this, there will come a time when, no matter how hard you pull and lean, you cannot get as far wide of the boat as you need to increase your angle. Now is the moment to learn the counter cut.

The counter cut

To gain maximum power into the ramp you need to start your cut at right angles to the boat pylon. And the only way you can obtain that position is by swinging there from the left of the boat in a giant pendulum motion. Pull out to the left of the boat as wide as you can and settle in the correct skiing position. When you are about 100 yds (100 m) from the ramp (this will vary from skier to skier) turn and accelerate hard across the wake towards the boat.

After you have crossed the second wake give a final pull, flatten off the edges and lift the right ski. You are now 'coasting'. Again the reduction in drag will speed you round the right side of the boat and, in advanced cases, place you a yard or so in front of the boat pylon.

Expert skiers let go of the handle with the right hand as they coast and extend their left towards the boat. They also arch their bodies, putting their skis as far away from the boat as possible. These two actions help take in potential slack rope as they begin their turn as well as giving more pivoting power.

Use the extended left arm as a 'slack rope gauge'. There should always be a slight pull on that arm. If there isn't you have slack rope and must correct it by aiming your skis away from the boat.

Replace your raised ski on the water as you round the boat and continue coasting on two skis.

Do not swing beyond the bow, that will only pull you back towards the boat. Aim instead to attain that position in front of the pylon as you reach boat speed – and then turn your skis towards the wake. In the time it takes to turn the skis, you will have dropped back and be perfectly placed in line with the pylon.

As you turn, pull the handle in, grabbing hold with the right hand again and edging towards the ramp. The turn should be controlled, with acceleration building all the way to the ramp. This means you will need to force the arms in harder the nearer you get to the ramp, with more weight and power going through the right ski.

Crushing is the most common fault at this stage for two reasons:

1 The additional impetus as you hit the ramp.
2 You are late setting yourself for the jump.

Nothing can cure the first point except experience. The second is simple to put right. Set yourself for the jump as you turn. In other words, if the ramp was suddenly moved into the middle of the wake you would still be ready for it. Just get into position as you start the cut, brace yourself and hold it.

Theoretically, you don't pull, you just hold your arms in and down to take the pull in your most powerful position. If your arms go out you will lose your edge, lean and direction and you are asking for trouble to continue with the jump.

A lot of skiers trying this advanced cut for the first time tend to relax their pull as they come into the ramp. If you do release the pull – and

Hello out there! Karen Morse, Britain's European champion, shows just how wide of the boat you need to go on the counter cut

Rick McCormick, US world champion, lifts a ski on the counter cut.

even world-class skiers continue to do so – you will bank in the air. This is not dangerous as it can be corrected by simply winging the bodyweight the other way, but distance is sacrificed because a lot of pull in the air is lost.

Headwind, tailwind and crosswind

In a headwind counter cut stronger and later and crouch a little on the skis: stronger because the wind prevents you from getting out; later because you cannot coast so easily.

In a tailwind counter cut sooner and not as strongly as usual for the opposite reasons.

If you are cutting into a crosswind, cut harder. If you are cutting *with* a crosswind allow it to do some of the work.

Wayne Grimditch (USA) snow ploughing

Snow ploughing

This is an advanced manoeuvre which slows you down if you have counter cut too late and come level with the boat too early. Push down with both inside edges and bring the front of the feet together to make a V. This should be used only if you have completely misjudged the cut. In most cases, lowering the raised ski will slow you down sufficiently.

If your counter cut is too early, keep the raised ski up for longer and the decrease in drag will speed you through.

Flight

There should be no alteration of your position when you are in the air. Keep the skis flat. It may seem that the air will catch under the front tips and make you buoyant if you raise them. So it will – but it will also drag against the back tips.

Keep both hands on the handle to maintain the pull through the air until you are so advanced that you are landing fairly wide of the boat and the pull on landing comes directly from the right side. Then you should release the left hand and extend the right arm towards the boat

Rick McCormick (USA) above, and Mike Hazelwood (GB) below, show super form – arms in and down, body slightly forward, legs straight and eyes judging landing spot. The perfect way to fly as Mike Hazelwood (GB) shows ideal form in the air

The author comes in for a perfect two-point landing.

as you come into the landing. If your take-off is faulty you can try to get into position by gently shifting your weight in the air.

As you start double-cutting, you should also begin looking down to judge landings. You will be reaching heights of near 10 ft and the floating sensation makes you lose your perspective.

Raising the ramp

In my opinion, men should be skiing at 30 mph (48 kmph) over the 5 ft (1·50 m) ramp, double-cutting and jumping 80–100 ft (25–30 m) before raising the ramp to their maximum 6 ft (1·80 m). There is a big difference in these two ramps – far greater than moving from 4 ft to 5 ft (1·20 m to 1·50 m). The angle on a 6 ft (1·80 m) ramp is 20 degrees and you are literally thrown up into the air. Unless you are completely ready for the transfer you could frighten yourself all over again.

First jump in the 1975 world championships . . . the author is looking good, but eventually misjudged the landing with dire results

Only a few minutes later he is in mid-air during his second jump. The left knee is already swelling ominously

Wayne Grimditch (USA) preparing to land wide of the boat, eyes fixed on the water

Wayne Grimditch, US world champion, lands perfectly and looks back at the boat to get a rough idea of his distance

Arm sling

A device which should be used by experts alone as it is effective only when you are jumping around 150 ft (45 m) off a 6 ft (1·80 m) ramp or, in the case of a woman, 110 ft (33 m) off a 5 ft (1·50 m) ramp. It is then you start to get the really big pull on the ramp and in the air and an arm sling helps keep the arms in to make full use of that pull. It is really a strap which binds one arm or the other to the body. I always wear it round my left arm because if the left arm stays in you are far more likely to remain square. A right-arm sling can pull the upper body towards the boat. The only disadvantage of the left-arm sling is that you cannot extend that arm so fully when you are coasting to the right of the boat after the counter cut. With a right-arm sling your powers of recovery in the air are limited because the right arm is the one holding the handle and full extension is sometimes needed to maintain good balance.

Jump measurement

A competition jump is calculated by three sets of meters, mounted alongside the course at strategic points. There are two meters at each point, and two meter readers. Each fixes the sights of the meter on the heel of the skis as the skier lands and then reads off the angle. These are fed back to a master board which geometrically works out the length of the jump. The skier can roughly judge his distance by the relation of his landing to the boat. If he is level with the front of the boat off a 6 ft (1·80 m) ramp, he has jumped more than 160 ft (50 m), the pylon 150 ft (45 m), the stern 140 ft (40 m).

In competition each skier has three jumps and for an attempt to be valid he must ski out upright past another buoy 328 ft (100 m) beyond the ramp.

5 *Boat driving*

Driving a boat and driving one with a waterskier on the end is as different as motoring in a mini instead of an articulated truck.

Suddenly the boat is not just, say, 16 ft (5 m) long. There is an extra 75 ft (23 m) stretching way out the back with somebody hanging on to the end. What should be simple things like turning corners take on the complexity of geometrical theorems.

Boat driving is as difficult as, if not more difficult than, learning to waterski itself. It took me all of five years before I felt fully competent and I was no weekend-only enthusiast.

The boat driver is the most important person in waterskiing; navigator, co-ordinator and, when on the water, the final arbitrator. Without him nothing happens.

Indeed, a good boat driver is a precious commodity, to be respected and cosseted, bought drinks for in the bar and generally made to feel that he should never stray away from your club. He holds the key to success or failure for beginners and the difference between an afternoon of joy or sheer misery for the more advanced skier.

Besides having eyes in the back of his head, the good boat driver needs to obey five basic rules:

1 Understand his boat's capabilities.
2 Understand the skier's capabilities.
3 Know the area in which he is driving.
4 Know the correct procedures and regulations.
5 Follow the safety code.

1 Understand the boat's capabilities

A big, powerful waterski boat is a very potent piece of machinery and will easily run away with you if you do not respect it. But no matter what size boat you have you should always be well aware of its various idiosyncrasies before attempting to pull a skier. Learn where all the controls are so you could find them blindfolded; you will have more than enough to do when you are on the water to waste time groping around for one instrument or another. Ensure that the driving position is comfortable and that all-round visibility is unimpaired.

2   Understand the skier's capabilities

Thirty miles per hour will be slow to one skier, an invitation to a nervous breakdown for another. Examine the credentials of each skier before taking them out, their experience, age, size, level of performance.

3   Know the skiing area

Find out the water depth in the skiing area and around the landing jetty. Check for unusual current flows and submerged obstacles. Inspect the area before the first run and double check at regular intervals for floating hazards and flotsam.

4   Know the correct procedures and regulations

The British Water Ski Federation publishes full lists of regulations for the use of boats in different types of waters. For instance, if you are operating around coastal areas you should learn the regulations appertaining to crowded waters.

Never ski without an observer in the boat. He can watch the skier all the time and allow you to concentrate on the difficult job in hand. Make sure that you understand the signals the skier will use. It is the only way you can talk to each other once you leave the jetty.

5   Follow the safety code

It is the boat driver's responsibility to ensure that the skier is wearing a life jacket, a helmet for jumping and the correct type of skis. The coastal and river boat should also carry enough life jackets for everyone on board, plus a fire extinguisher, bailing can, paddle and anchor. It is preferable to carry only one passenger in the boat, otherwise conversations spring up and that can be distracting.

Starts can be extremely hazardous. In a deep-water start ensure that the ski tips are above the water and that the tow rope is taut from the pylon right down to the handle. Wait for the skier's signal and then give him a smooth, steady take-off.

On dock starts make sure that the coiled rope is in clear view. When the skier falls close down the throttle immediately and return to the skier at idling speed. That way you are totally in control, there is no danger to the skier and no wake disturbance is left across your path. Approach the fallen skier on the driver's side, that way you can see him all the time and there is less risk of hitting him with the boat or propeller. Take the wind into account and always come into the skier so the wind is blowing you away from him. And be careful not to run over the tow rope. Of course, if the skier has fallen and not given the clasped hand signal you must return to him as quickly as possible. But whatever the situation *never* take a skier on board without shutting off the engine. It is easy to nudge the throttle and send the boat storming forward while you are engaged helping the skier into the boat.

Always operate the boat from the driver's seat and not the side. It's tempting to sit on the side to catch the breeze or get a better view, but believe me, it's dangerous. I've seen boats hit a sudden wave, tip the driver off the side and then go careering out of control into the bank. Don't allow anybody else to sit on the side, or back, of the boat either. They can get a ducking the same way and if they fall from the back of the boat the chances are the skier will run into them.

Always try to distribute the weight evenly on both sides of the boat, that gives a uniform wake and is most satisfactory for the skier.

Beginners

Beginners are by far the hardest skiers to drive. There is so much manoeuvring involved. But always remember, you've got the control, they haven't. It is up to you to be patient and handle every stage slowly and steadily.

Conversely, you must be ready to react instantaneously on the throttle especially as the beginner struggles to prepare himself for the initial tug. He may call ready, and the boat driver surges away just as he loses his balance for the umpteenth time. The good driver should be prepared, throttle back immediately and wait for him to settle once more.

Up and away

Once up on the water, the most important factors are speed and direction. All movement of the throttle must be smooth and gradual. Direction should be as straight as possible to give the skier a regular wake. Maintain the same line on the return run to keep water disturbance to a minimum.

When turning, go out of the course on the turn and come back into the course on the straight. That gives the skier a longer straight run to

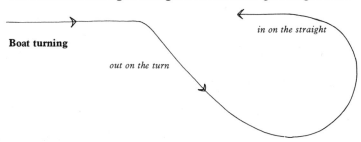

Boat turning

out on the turn

in on the straight

get settled – especially when he is tackling slalom, tricks or jumps.

Establish a regular pattern every time you drive then others will be able to anticipate your movements.

Every time you turn check the skier's position either through your rear-view mirror or with a quick glance over your shoulder. Never attempt to turn if the skier is cutting sharply outside the wake on either side of the boat. If he is cutting to the inside of your turn he will have insufficient speed to stay on the water and a small boat, banking for the turn, can be capsized by the sudden drag of a sinking skier. If he is cutting away from your turn, the whiplash rope effect will give him a sudden, mighty surge of speed.

Always attempt to turn in such a way that the skier is in full control and on the edges of his skis. The better the ski, the faster the turns. And if you are forced into a sudden, emergency turn, chop the throttle and dunk the skier.

Docking

Docking a boat is one of the most skilful manoeuvres and should be practised repeatedly. To start with, use a buoy as a dummy dock and perfect it in such a way that you do not have to rely on reverse – that is your brake and should be used only as a last resort.

Slalom

Perfect direction and an almost 'sixth sense' feel of the throttle are essential for the good slalom driver. The buoys are positioned equidistant from the centre of the boat's course so any deviation in line will destroy the skier's timing, especially in short-rope slalom. The feel of the throttle, too, is critical because the skier will be exerting tremendous pulls as he rounds each buoy and the driver has to know exactly how much gas to give to compensate for each pull and keep the speed right.

In fact, there are three ways a driver can tackle a slalom course:

1 He can go into the course too fast and allow the skier's pulling power to bring the average speed down to the regulation. This requires little throttle control during the run and is by far the least satisfactory for the skier. He is taken racing into the first two buoys and is virtually at a standstill by the sixth.
2 He can go into the course at the correct speed and tweak the throttle just enough to compensate for the skier's pull at each buoy. This is the ideal rhythm but it can also be achieved only by the best drivers. And if it is done badly it is even worse for the skier than the first method.
3 He can go in at the correct speed and increase the revs during the pull through the gate and round the first buoy *only*. Minor speed adjustments can be made at each buoy but nothing like as definite as in method No 2. This last version is the best for the majority of drivers because it provides a solid run for the skier without requiring a too advanced driving technique.

You can gauge your speed through the slalom course either by the rev-counter or the aquameter (speedometer). Judging by revs should be reserved for the experts because the readings are so totally different when one is not pulling a skier that they take a lot of mental adjustment when one is. Aquameters are operated by the flow of water under the boat and will vary fractionally as the skier pulls and banks the boat. A fluctuation between 35½ mph (57 kmph) and 36½ mph (59 kmph) will mean an average speed of 36 mph (58 kmph). Also some aquameters react more slowly than others. Get used to yours.

The speed to time scale for slalom is:

Mph	Time (secs.)	Tolerance (secs.)
30 (49 kmph)	19	18·8–19·7
32 (52 kmph)	17·8	17·6–18·3
34 (55 kmph)	17	16·7–17·3
36 (58 kmph)	16·1	15·9–16·3

Tricks

Trick skiing is the most individual of the three disciplines and, as such, the driver must cater for every whim of the skier. Every skier has his own tricking speed and it doesn't matter whether you think he is right or wrong, what he says goes.

When he gives signals to increase or decrease speed react with a definite twist of the throttle so he knows his signal has been under-stood and acted upon. I have seen keyed-up skiers become irate because they believe the driver was ignoring them when in fact his change had merely been too smooth. Change speed by at least half a mile an hour on the first instruction. If that is too much or too little, halve the difference.

Trick skiing is such a sudden-death affair that the skier must be given as long as possible to get used to the boat speed, wake and rope length. Although the speed should be perfect all the way through the approach, it will still be necessary to throttle up a fraction to offset the sudden pull as the skier starts to trick. Certain tricks, such as the 540 front to back wake turn, will exert powerful pulls while others, like the modest side slide, are more sedate. Dropping a ski also brings a sudden increase in drag.

In these cases, it is far better to overcompensate. Coming out of a trick too fast is far more acceptable to skiers than coming out too slowly.

Remember: When a skier falls during a run do not power turn the boat as that will only cause disturbance.

Jumping

Driving for jumping is the most crucial test of skill of them all because a mistake here could cause injury; errors in slalom and tricks usually mean nothing more than a fall or mistake.

The better the skier, the better the driver must be. An expert jump skier is travelling in excess of 60 mph (100 kmph) and needs somebody at the other end who knows exactly what they are doing.

Ask the skier personally what speed he requires and what distance away from the ramp the boat's path should be.

On the run to the approach keep the boat speed two or three miles per hour below the skier's request, checking regularly that he is prepared. Build the speed as you come out of the turn so that when you start the run the throttle is set and will need no further adjustment until the skier starts the counter cut.

The driver must anticipate the skier's pull and tweak the throttle an instant before the skier starts his cut. Many skiers pull extremely hard and the extra speed needed to maintain par may be considerable. As the skier reaches the widest point of his cut the pull will decrease and the throttle must be adjusted accordingly. The skier will now be coasting as he prepares for the decisive cut into the ramp and there is no excuse whatsoever for not having the correct speed. Jumping at advanced level especially is all about split-second timing and aiming at tiny targets.

After the skier hits the ramp the pull will come off totally – and then snap back on with a vengeance as he lands.

6 *Equipment*

Skis

The safest rule when buying your first pair of skis is: make the sales assistant's life hell. Make sure he knows what he's talking about by asking plenty of questions, look at as many pairs as possible and then, if you're not 100 per cent satisfied, shop elsewhere. Don't be fobbed off. Skis are an expensive purchase.

They are the most essential pieces of equipment you need to waterski – and the most individual. Personal preference, not complicated technical data, is the major guide line. Simply go for the ones which sound as if they fit all your requirements. I can help in the decision only with a few tips:

Beginners

Design is not important for beginners. But size is. If the skis are too large they will be hard to control; too small and you will use a lot of extra energy maintaining balance.

The size-weight scale is roughly:

Inches	Pounds
60 (152 cm)	100 (45 kg)
62 (157 cm)	125 (56 kg)
64 (162 cm)	150 (68 kg)
66 (167 cm)	175 (79 kg)
68 (172 cm)	200 (90 kg)
70 (177 cm)	225 (102 kg)

Skis are made from either wood, fibreglass or aluminium. To start with you should ignore fibreglass and aluminium as they are far harder to handle than wooden skis and are usually twice as expensive.

Beginners' skis come in two varieties of shape – square backed and tapered. Square-backed skis give greater flotation and are good for skiers who just want a bit of fun. But those who are keen to progress would be better advised to buy tapered skis as they are a little more advanced and convert easily into a combination pair. A combination pair has one of the skis fitted with a double binding ready for mono-skiing. Personally, I feel it is better to pay that little bit extra and buy a combination pair from the start.

Ensure the ski is straight or curves up slightly. Some manufacturers, for reasons known only to themselves, produce water skis which bend downwards in the style of snow skis. The tip is dragged under and the skier falls.

Bindings should be supple. If they are cardboard stiff because cheap rubber has been used, they will be most uncomfortable, rip more easily and could also cause injury by failing to release your foot quickly enough in the event of a fall.

Brightly coloured skis have the advantage of being quickly spotted in the water. If the ones you choose are dark, paint at least the tips in a conspicuous colour.

Slalom skis

The great danger in buying a slalom ski is that people come in after their first successful run and say 'O.K. what's the most advanced ski you've got?' It's like passing your driving test in the morning and then buying a seven-litre sports car in the afternoon.

Don't be too ambitious, there are plenty of very good in-between skis. It may seem like an unnecessary expense not to go straight for the 'super ski' but it need not be. A well-cared-for ski will maintain its value for years.

flat with and without bevel   *grooved*   *concave*

Flat, grooved and concave cross-sections

There are three main types of slalom ski:
1 flat, 2 grooved, 3 concave.

Flat Excellent for general skiing, such as having a good time at the seaside. But if you are keen to progress you will soon outgrow it. As you learn to turn harder and faster, so the flat ski will start to skip out.

Remember – all combination skis are flat, so there is no point buying a flat slalom ski if you invested in a combination pair at the start. Obvious, I know, but some people do.

Grooved This is the ski I would recommend as the in-between step for most skiers. The grooves, running the length of each ski, give increased traction for acceleration, deceleration and turning power. This ski bites the water well without posing too many tricky handling problems. It will allow you to tackle the slalom course with a fair degree of authority but falls just short of competition level.

Concave A concave ski is like an inverted gutter and it bites the water without losing turning power. Just how deeply it bites depends on the type you buy.

There are three main varieties, each with its own special characteristics: 1 edge to edge, 2 tunnel, 3 standard concave.

Before I discuss those, it is time to talk about *rocker, flex* and *edge* – the three most important properties of a ski. Rocker is the bend in the ski from tip to tip and does three things: it keeps the tip out of the water; it gives the drag necessary for deceleration and it aids turning. Just how much rocker a ski should have is a critical question as an excess will hinder acceleration.

Rocker should be built throughout the entire length of the ski, increasing as it travels to the back. Don't buy skis with all the rocker at the back and flat at the front – that brings the tip uncomfortably close to the water.

Flex is the 'give' in the ski from tip to tip. Too much flex allows the ski to flap about in rough and causes the rocker to increase to an excess. An over-flexed ski will be very fast in the turn but poor on acceleration. Too little flex has the opposite effect.

Edge gives the bite needed for turning, accelerating and decelerating. The bottom edge of the ski should either be rounded or – as I prefer – angled at 45 degrees.

Rounded and 45° edges

rounded   *45°*

EDGE TO EDGE   Edge to edge concave skis turn and bite really hard, but they are difficult to handle. Your weight distribution must be near perfect or you are heading for trouble. There is rarely such a thing as a smooth ride with edge to edge skis. It's all fits and starts at a furious pace.

TUNNEL   Riding on a tunnel ski is like running on rails. You work your arms, lean . . . and the ski does the rest. It's a nice, smooth ride but with less power and less bite.

STANDARD CONCAVE   The majority of good skiers use this type. It is a cross between the previous two. It turns well, bites well and accelerates and decelerates effectively without being outstanding at any.

Edge to edge, tunnel, standard skis

As always, though, the choice of ski is totally a matter of personal preference. Rick McCormick, the American world champion, uses edge to edge; Robbi Zucchi, Italy's maestro of the slalom, uses tunnel and I swear by complete concave.

Bindings

The bindings on the slalom ski are also very much an individual thing. The further back the bindings, the faster you will turn, but your balance must also be more perfect. Test the bindings in various positions before deciding, but wherever you finally place them remember that both feet must be close together.

Personally, I prefer the bindings forward on the ski because that way you get slowish turns and hard pulls – and that's the slalom technique I enjoy. Also you are less likely to tip over the front of the ski . . . a fact an enormous number of skiers don't appreciate. They reason that the further back the binding the less likely they are to be pulled forward. They forget that the further back they go, the more sudden and vicious the pull will be out of each buoy – and it is that pull which yanks them over the tip.

I also prefer the rear binding to be in the form of a strip, rather than a complete binding, for two reasons: it is harder to do a deep-water start with both feet in the ski and, second, if you are tugged forwards during the run and your back heel is forced up it is impossible to get it 100 per cent flat down on the ski again if it is encased in a complete binding.

Fins

Many competition skiers drill holes in their slalom ski fins to aid deceleration by using water pressure. I have sixteen holes in mine and it actually whistles as I round the buoys.

Finally, try and pick a ski which complements your bad turning side. I used one for years which made my bad turn worse but gave me an excellent good turn. Consequently I became a very one-sided skier for several years.

Trick skis

Whereas a good slalom skier is always on the look-out to discover a better ski, the trick skier usually selects a pair he finds most comfortable and sticks with them. Design has changed dramatically over the years, but the priority is still to choose trick skis which 'feel' right for you.

By necessity trick skis have to be stiff so that they track well with the minimum of drag. This used to mean that they were heavy, wooden contraptions. The introduction of fibreglass brought a revolution; the essential stiffness remains, but the weight has been cut by half and it is not by chance that trick records have been rewritten over the past few years.

Trick skis come in two main categories: short and wide and long and narrow. Short, wide skis turn more smoothly and with less effort. Their extra width also provides a more stable platform. They are the most commonly used these days because in recent years the accent has

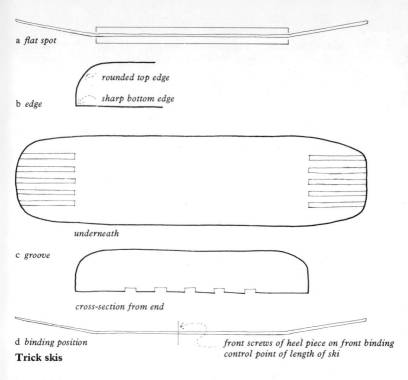

a *flat spot*

b *edge*
- *rounded top edge*
- *sharp bottom edge*

c *groove*

underneath

cross-section from end

d *binding position*   *front screws of heel piece on front binding*
                       control point of length of ski

Trick skis

been high-scoring toe-hold tricks which call for constant spinning on the water.

Long, narrow skis give greater traction and so perform faster because you are not sliding about between tricks. These were fashionable a few years back when the emphasis was on wake turns. Both sorts of skis come with either rounded ends or square ends. As you would expect, rounded ends make turning more effortless, square ends aid traction.

As I have said, it is all a matter of personal preference, but as a general rule beginners would be advised to buy short, wide skis with square ends. Then they have the best of both worlds – a bit of slide and a bit of traction on skis which aren't too tiring to handle.

Grooves   Some trick skis have grooves running along their undersides at each end. They are usually about 8 in (20 cm) long, ¼ in (0·6 cm) wide and ⅛ in (0·3 cm) deep. Sometimes there are as many as eight per ski. These have been added to give greater traction and are not too common these days.

Edges   The bottom edge of a trick ski must be sharp, the top edge must be rounded. The sharp edge is there to bite the water and give plenty of grip, especially when you are cutting into the wake. The rounded top edge will pull the ski back out of the water should it dive under. Test it for yourself by holding the back of a spoon under a tap. The stream of water running down both sides pulls the spoon upwards; the same applies to waterskis.

Flat spot   All trick skis need a flat spot. Otherwise the continuous rocker causes drag.

Bindings   Amazingly, the majority of manufacturers persist in putting the bindings in the wrong place and that is half the reason why people fall so many times while tricking. In my opinion, the front screw of the horseshoe which secures the heel binding should be in the middle of the ski's length.

I also believe that when tricking on one ski the back foot should be at an angle of 45 degrees across the ski and close to the front foot. This gives the most natural balancing position without costing anything in spinning power.

Size chart   The approximate size-weight scale is:

Juniors: 36–40 in (98 cm)
Up to 160 lb (68 kg): 40 in (100 cm)
Up to 200 lb (90 kg): 42 in (106 cm)
Over 200 lb (90 kg): 44 in (112 cm)

Jump skis

Like trick skis, jump skis also come in short and long versions. The smaller skis are very easy to manoeuvre but generate less speed; the larger skis are very fast but harder to handle. Again the choice is yours; I went for manoeuvrability.

But whatever you decide make sure the skis have a continuous rocker. This is essential, otherwise when you flatten off the tip will be sucked down by the water. Too much rocker is also to be avoided as that will create drag and cost you all-important speed.

Medium flex is best; too much and the skis will bend and drag during the cut; too little and the skis will jar excessively on hitting the ramp and landing.

Binding   The easy way to check if the binding is in the correct place on a jump ski is to pick it up holding just the flap of the front section of the binding between your fingers. The ski should hang parallel to the ground or, at most, with a slight upward tilt.

Size chart   The approximate size-weight scale is:

Juniors: 63 in (160 cm)
Up to 160 lb (72·5 kg): 66 in (167 cm)
Over 160 lb (72·5 kg): 69 in (175 cm)

Care of skis

Skis should be stored in a moderate temperature and preferably on a rack. Wooden skis will warp if left in the sun and can become brittle if allowed to dry out completely. Keep them well varnished with a hard, clear polyurethane. Fibreglass skis must be constantly checked for chips and cracks – especially jump skis. Fill any small chips immediately before they can spread. Care of skis will be repaid over and over again, both on the water and in your wallet.

Wood or fibreglass?

This, as they say, is the 64,000-dollar question and there is no easy answer. If you find a good wooden ski which suits your requirements, it is a thing of beauty. The problem is that no two wooden skis are the same. I once had what were supposed to be identical wooden slalom skis. One was a dream, the other a complete pig.

Every piece of wood varies from the next in density and that affects the rocker and flex. They are machined and so will differ fractionally every time. Also wooden skis are sensitive to temperature and conditions. They can warp, change shape, lose part of their rocker, become more or less flexible. Fibreglass skis, on the other hand, are constant. They come from a mould and one fibreglass ski will not be an iota different from the next one out of that mould or the millionth.

If you find a good fibreglass ski which suits you, you can sleep nights. With wood the thought of damage or theft is a nightmare.

Wet suits

These are worn for warmth and protection. They are normally made from neoprene, a rubber containing myriads of tiny little air holes, and lined by nylon. The principle is that a thin layer of water should seep inside between the body and the suit, become warm and then act as insulation. Because of this a wet suit must fit as snugly as possible without becoming restrictive. If it is too loose great bucketfuls of water will rush inside and you will freeze.

The neoprene comes in differing thicknesses from 2 mm through to 8 mm for sub-zero underwater diving. For waterskiing 3 mm is best as it provides a fine level of warmth without too much restriction.

A *shorty* wet suit comprising vest and shorts is an in-between outfit for skiing in warm weather – or in competition where fuller flexibility is needed.

Dry suit

These are made from very thin rubber, the same sort of thickness as car inner tubes. They are one-piece suits with rubber seals at the neck, ankles and wrists. They are completely watertight, but give little

113

warmth; the idea is to ski with clothes on underneath, like a tracksuit. They are baggy and inclined to flap in the wind so they are not ideal for slalom and jumping. But they are great time-savers and also enable skiers to train throughout the coldest winters.

Life jackets

This is a misnomer really because the life jackets used in waterskiing are no more than flotation devices. They will keep you floating on the water but they will not tip you onto your back in true life-saving style. They are made from either nylon or foam. The foam ones are inclined to rip very easily and rarely last for more than a couple of seasons.

There are two types: normal and jump jacket. The normal version has shoulder straps; the jump jacket gives full protection to the shoulders and can be restrictive for slalom and trick skiing.

Gloves

These are made from vinyl-impregnated cotton and are almost identical to golf gloves. Indeed, skiers I know tote a handy six iron in their ski gloves and vice versa. Gloves partly protect hands from the almost obligatory callouses, but their main function is to improve grip. They are essential at the top end of skiing – I remember I once went out for a slalom without them and couldn't do a thing.

Boots and hoods

These offer warmth and protection on cold days, although boots should not be worn when attempting toe-hold tricks. They can easily stick in the strap.

Helmets

The main purpose of a helmet is to protect you from flying skis so it does not need to be a heavy, cumbersome affair like the ones worn by motorcyclists. A lightweight helmet made from reinforced plastic is adequate and sensible; a heavy helmet will make your head dip as you hit the ramp and as you land, therefore increasing the chances of crushing. The helmet should protect the ears as well but it must not fit too tightly across them otherwise your sense of balance will be impaired. The helmet rim must have holes in it to allow the water to run through, otherwise the helmet will 'bucket' every time you fall and it could deliver a painful blow to your face. For the same reason you should choose one with a chin strap rather than one that fastens round the neck. A chin strap will allow the helmet to fall off under pressure. A neck strap merely allows it to slip forward. I know – I broke my nose the last time I wore a neck strap.

Handles

Handles come in a vast variety, ranging from the plainest wood to expertly designed foam rubber luxury. The cheaper ones are hard on the hands, especially when you start to ski well and are pulling something like 300 lb (136 kg) and more. The foam rubber also supplies a solid grip.

Handles come in two main sizes: 11 in (27·94 cm) and 15 in (38·1 cm) long. The short handle is mandatory for slalom and jumps but some people prefer the long one for tricks. I disagree with them. There is a tendency to become lazy when tricking with a long handle; there is so much more to aim for that you don't try so hard to reach it. With the short handle you *have* to aim to almost touch your other hand as you grip the handle. Also I find the short handle far easier to manoeuvre for steps and toe-hold tricks.

Toe-holds

These are made from either leather, rubber or canvas. The canvas are the crudest of all – and in my experience the best. They grip the foot really well without being too abrasive and always give perfect release. The toe-hold fits into the handle in such a way that a quick tug on the handle or extreme pressure such as a fall, frees the foot.

Rope

Braided polypropylene has proved to be the best skiing rope. It is very strong and light with a minimum of stretch and it floats on water. The specified size for slalom and jumping is ⅜ in (0·95 cm). Trick skiing requires a more solid line to minimise stretch and ⅝ in (1·58 cm) is recommended. If it is too thick and heavy it will sway around.

Boats

As I said elsewhere, any size of boat will suffice provided it has enough power to pull someone out of the water, but ideally a waterski boat should be more than 200 horse power and at least 16 ft (4·8 m) long. I prefer inboards to outboards because they respond more ideally for the sport. They have a solid grip on the water whereas an outboard tends to flit on the surface. Also the wake from an outboard is smaller and choppier in the middle, which is unsuitable for tricks.

There are three leading makes of recognised inboard ski boats – the Boesch from Switzerland and the American Correct Craft and Master Craft. The Boesch is the 'saloon car' giving a smooth, steady ride and ideal wake and is the best to ski behind. But the other two, the 'sports cars' are more responsive and designed to give comfort for the driver during long teaching stints.

But whatever you choose, go for a hand throttle. They react quicker

Bridle

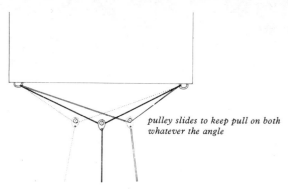

*pulley slides to keep pull on both
whatever the angle*

than foot throttles. Keep it well oiled, the damp will cause it to stiffen up. You will also need an aquameter and a large rear-view mirror.

The ski pylon should be near the back of the boat on an outboard and in the middle of the boat on an inboard. It is essential only for good skiers where a huge pull is being exerted. For others a pulley fixed on a bridle on the back of the boat is quite adequate.

7 Making a champion

Champions come in two categories: those who want to get to the top and those who need to. The need-to-be champions are the proverbial hungry fighters, the people with something to prove.

Many of the greatest champions have come from this category: Jesse Owens, the black track star from white America; Murray Halberg, the New Zealander who overcame polio to win an Olympic gold medal; Rocky Graziano, who rose from the slums of New York to the world middleweight title; even Lester Piggott, the greatest of all jockeys who is beset by a speech impediment.

In my own, more modest, way, I was that sort of champion – a shy, self-conscious Yorkshire boy who needed desperately to prove himself. Once I had discovered waterskiing I was totally committed to becoming the best. It was dedication of the purest sort, but at that time I wasn't even sure what the word meant.

I was a late starter at the age of thirteen. These days, with competition becoming fiercer every year, a potential champion must be on the water by the time he is ten. That way he will have completed the greater part of his vital, rudimentary training while distractions such as girlfriends and discothèques are filed under 'pending'.

He needs to start young, secondly, because the teens and early twenties have proved to be the zenith of a skier's career. That is the age he is at his most agile – and adaptable. As he grows that bit longer in the tooth his increased strength and experience will compensate in part for his diminishing suppleness. But only in part and it is always those mini-fractions of excellence which win the major honours.

Having said that, though, there is no excuse whatsoever for pressurising young skiers. One of the most disconcerting sounds at ski areas is small children being bullied into going on the water. The whole point about waterskiing is that it is a sport and as such is meant to be enjoyed – no matter what the aspirations of the child's parents or coach. Once we lose sight of that we may as well pack up and move to Russia.

To start with, children should concentrate on trick skiing and mono-skiing. At their tender age these are the easiest ways of having fun on the water; and the more they enjoy it the more time they will want to spend doing it.

I do not recommend letting a child jump until he is at least thirteen, by which time he will have developed enough to withstand the strain without fear of injury. His slalom will also be fairly frustrating and unexciting until he has the necessary strength to take the pull correctly. But he can trick ski competently no matter how small and weak . . . and this is what youngsters should concentrate on.

It all starts to happen around the age of thirteen to fourteen. The body has grown enough to handle the unique stresses and the brain is sufficiently experienced to cope with most eventualities.

I was fifteen when I won my first title – the British junior championship – and the following year I won the north European junior championship. Until that breakthrough my skiing had been unspectacular; then it all came right as my physique and technique amalgamated.

Training for waterskiing, like any other sport, is time-consuming and, at times, tedious. There is a great possibility that the dedicated waterskier will become totally self-centred and indeed he must if he is to reach the top. What is wrong, though, is if he allows that dedication to sour him as a human being – or if he allows the sport to take over his life to the exclusion of all else. It is essential to have a relaxation and whether it is collecting match-box tops or girlfriends it must form an important part of your existence. Then, when things go wrong with your skiing, as they surely will, it is not the end of the world. Well, not quite anyway.

As for becoming 'sour' as a person . . . I have always abided by the principle that being a champion is not enough. You must aim to be a good one. That may sound like an old-fashioned, agonising cliché but I believe it is the cornerstone of sport. You must win and lose with equal grace and both are hard to do. Don't confuse good manners with weakness, though. A killer instinct is an essential part of the champion's make-up. Never sit on that jetty thinking, 'Well, if it goes wrong this time there's always next week.' Sometimes there isn't. You have to aim to go out every time and blast the opposition off the face of the water. With a good-natured smile, of course.

Coaching

Coaches are very much a question of personal taste. I was extremely fortunate to be discovered by an Austrian called Rainer Kolb. Under his guidance my skiing was transformed. He had this happy knack of spotting faults and in my case finding instant remedies. Most importantly we talked on the same wavelength. A coach can be technically brilliant but if for some reason you and he don't communicate you are better off finding someone you can talk to even though their talent may be inferior. In the long run you will benefit.

There is a great temptation with a good coach to rely on him totally. I have made the mistake myself of mothering skiers and then have watched in dismay as they have looked bewildered and lost once they are on their own. The skier must think for himself; disagreement and discussion are so important to advancement because what is perfect for one skier may be all wrong for another.

It is not wise, either, to model yourself on good skiers. Everybody does something unorthodox; world champions like Liz Allen and Bruce Cockburn go against the textbook 50 per cent of the time. That is because they have worked out time-saving contractions, or have found a certain style that suits their own peculiarities. Try to be as orthodox as possible to begin with, then as you go along you will find your own short cuts and improvements.

At the same time, though, do not be afraid to seek the advice of a good skier. They may seem aloof but everyone I know derives great pleasure from helping the less gifted.

Training

The first requisite for training is that it must be regular and that means going out whatever the weather and whatever the water conditions. The joys of waterskiing will seem very far removed on some freezing mornings as you clamber into your wet suit but the sense of achievement afterwards will be immense. This is self-discipline and the reward is self-satisfaction.

It is advisable to train mainly with a boat driver you think is good at his job otherwise you will start off each time with a feeling of resentment. On the odd occasion, though, try a different driver for a session or two as this will stand you in good stead for the lucky dip aspect of competition. And if there is an observer in the boat don't make the mistake of showing off and performing to impress him. You're out there to improve your skiing not to provide free sideshows.

Your training timetable will depend on the climate you live in. Skiers in hot-weather countries can train on the water all the year round and it is highly advisable for the really serious skier to take a winter trip to somewhere like Florida for three months. But in cold-water countries like Britain and the majority of Europe a training routine would go like this:

October–May

Keep fit in a relaxed, enjoyable way. Jog about five miles four times a week to keep the weight down, play a couple of games of squash a week to stimulate agility and reflexes, and go swimming. You should maintain a fairly normal social life during this time, a few parties and, if you are old enough, a few beers. The worst thing for any waterskier is boredom and staleness. The heavy, committed training will come soon enough and he must go into it feeling relaxed and refreshed and eager.

Use this quieter period to build up your arms, back and stomach, the three most important physical areas for waterskiing. The best kind of arm exercises are pull ups which develop the biceps. *Push*-ups are not so useful as they aid the triceps which are hardly used in waterskiing. Sit-ups and torso raises are the simplest and most beneficial exercises for the stomach and back.

And the best warm-up manoeuvre immediately before taking to the water is a vigorous rolling of the arms, circling the elbows past the ears.

Do *not* attempt deep knee bends. These are bad for the joints at the best of times, but they are especially detrimental just before jumping as they cut off the blood supply momentarily and make the knee joints weaker, not stronger as so many people think.

The three categories of skiing need different qualities: tricks call for agility and controlled breathing; slalom needs bicep power; jumps need good old-fashioned guts.

May

This is the warm-up month when you are skiing unfit . . . and I would strongly advise against jumping during these first four weeks while your body is still adjusting to the strains of the sport.

The first week should go like this:

Monday　Warm up with a ten-minute jog and a set routine of stretching exercises. Then slalom once and trick twice, with plenty of recovery time between each session. The slalom, especially, will tire you enormously this early in the season and you should sleep soundly on the first night. Try to compact your training into one part of the day rather than spreading it throughout morning and afternoon. Too long between each outing on the water will cause stiffness . . . and your concentration is also bound to suffer. Build up to your slalom with easy speeds and remember that in tricks it is far better to put in ten minutes of concentrated work than a disjointed hour.

Tuesday　You'll be stiff from the previous day so make sure you warm up thoroughly before skiing. Then slalom once and trick twice as before. If you feel good, trick a third time.

Wednesday　The worst day of any season. You'll feel like death with every muscle shrieking. Slalom once and trick three times.

Thursday　It can only get better from now on. Your muscles should be responding less grudgingly. Slalom once and trick three times. Then a final slalom, if possible.

Friday　Slalom once and trick three times as before, but extend the slalom. This will probably happen automatically as your standard will be improving and you will be slaloming further. If you feel capable again, go onto the slalom course a second time so you have a thorough day's session. Do not overdo it, though. The important thing is to finish Friday tired, but not so tired that errors are coming into your skiing.

Saturday and Sunday　Rest.

Remainder of May　As first Friday.

June

From the start of June your daily routine should be one session of jumps (four attempts), two sessions of slalom, two sessions of tricks – *plus* one session of tricks or slalom depending upon which needs the practice most that particular day.

July

Jump, slalom and trick twice a day. But if your slalom is causing problems sacrifice a session of tricks to work on it and vice versa. On tricks, you should now be concentrating on perfecting your run but it is advisable to spend the odd few moments messing about learning new tricks because that will relieve the training monotony.

Build up to competition

In the week before competition perform each of the disciplines every day under competition conditions. If any of them let you down, do another session. If all three let you down write it off as a bad day and go home.

On the eve of competition I always went to bed at my normal time. Otherwise I would just have lain there getting twitchy. It is far better to be tired and sleep six hours than to lie awake in bed for twelve.

I liked to rise two hours before competition started and eat breakfast of cornflakes, eggs and coffee. Nothing too filling, but enough to fuel the system for the next few hours.

In the competition area I always sat apart from the other competitors where possible; too many of them try to psyche you out by commenting on the conditions, the boat driver and their own physical wellbeing. Instead I always sat somewhere I could watch the driver and see how he tackled the various courses. I liked to see his technique through the slalom and jump courses – and I always checked the judges' timing of the tricks run. Twenty seconds is the officially allotted time, but there can often be split-second delays before the gun is fired at the end. If this is happening consistently you can afford to be that fraction more deliberate with your run and make fewer mistakes.

Diet

Waterskiers burn energy at a furious rate and are therefore constantly hungry. But they must beware of overeating because bulk will affect mobility. Plenty of proteins like meat, milk, eggs, cheese and fresh vegetables are essential. A couple of days before strenuous competition a few extra potatoes and slices of bread will provide the carbohydrate store needed for instant energy.

Glossary

Apron
Safety arrangement on side of jump.

Arm sling
Device for keeping one or other arm close to the body in jumping, by means of strap around body and one around the arm strapped to it.

Backwash
Rough water caused by rebounding wake.

Balk
To refuse on approach to jump.

Bank
To swing skis away from boat while jumping and then back for landing. Normally not intentional.

Basics
Surface side-slides, 180s and 360s. Consist of eight tricks on two skis and sixteen tricks on one.

Bevel
Associated with edge of ski. An edge with bevel is not square. Various types – round, flat.

Binding
Holds foot to ski.

Blank/blade
Ski without binding.

Brake
Decelerate. Generally in slalom, but means same thing in jumping if counter cut is too fast.

Buoy
Marker in the water to guide skier or boat.

Coasting
Commonly used in jumping. After counter cut coast before double cut. Can coast on any skis – ski on flat skis without pull from boat. In slalom, coasting is bad – not decelerating effectively until on edge.

Concave
Design of ski to make it bite in water, hold in water. Different types – see edge to edge, tunnel.

Contestant buoy
Buoy which skier rounds.

Counter cut
Cut to set up position wide to right of boat for jumping. Start wide to left then cut to right.

Course
Where each event takes place.

Cow catcher
Same as Apron.

Crush
Opposite to Spring *or* Pop. *Body or legs are forced down.*

Cut
1 *To put ski on edge and spring out from the line of the boat.*
2 *See* Shortening.

Discipline
Event – slalom, trick or jump: term used at tournaments.

Dock
Platform into water which allows the boat to pick up the skier without beaching. (A water-skiing usage from the United States in place of the English word jetty.)

Double cut
Cut to the ramp from right of boat to left.

Drop ski
Ski discarded when learning mono. Also drop ski in tricks is the one left behind when going onto one.

Edge
In skiing – to edge is to put one edge deeper than other and cut. On skis – side of the ski.

Edge to edge
Type of concave, running across whole width of ski.

Event
Same as Discipline.

Figures
Another word for tricks event.

Fin
On bottom of ski to make it run true.

Flex
Amount of bend in a ski when under pressure.

Gas
Increase revs on boat to counteract pull from ski. (Most commonly heard in jumping.)

Gate
Two marker buoys for boat and skier to pass between on the slalom course; eight sets for boat, two sets for skier.

Grooves
In skis – slalom, tricks, and has even been tried in jumpers. Substitute for a fin on trick skis. Helps them all Track *better.*

Heel cup
Device used for purpose of keeping back foot from slipping out of binding.

Hit it
Term used by skier to signal to driver 'Go'; I don't like it as it can be misunderstood/misheard.

Hole
'In the hole' means the point where speed is slowest before accelerating out of turn.

Hook
Turn completed sharply.

Jam
Not Spring, *not* Crush – *resist.*

Jetty
Same as Dock.

Kick
Same as Spring, *or* Pop.

Line
1 *Skier's or boat's path.*
2 *Rope attaching skier to boat.*

Loop
Loops are in tow-rope for changing its length.

Mono
One ski, and so 'to mono'.

Non-skid pad
Sandpaper-type pad to stop foot sliding. Mainly used for back foot. Some competition skiers put them inside normal bindings.

Normal
The skier's favoured turn in tricks.

Pace
Speed at which tricks are performed.

Pass
1 *To pass is to refuse a jump.*
2 *Also used for a run in one direction in slalom.*

Pop
Spring, kick.

Preland
In jumping, to misjudge landing and resist while still in the air.

Programme
Personal sequence of tricks.

Progressive cut
Cut all the way to the ramp.

Pylon
The tow-rope can be attached to a pylon in the boat, instead of to the stern of the boat – necessary for advanced skiing.

Ramp
The take-off platform for the jump event.

Reach
Release with one hand and extend arm towards boat. Skier drops back from boat. When pulls in takes in slack rope.

Rear bridge
Strap-type binding for rear foot on slalom and trick ski.

Refuse
To Pass (1), *to* Balk.

Reverse
Opposite to Normal. *Not every trick has a reverse.*

Ride
A ski, a tow.

Rideout
Buoy which skier passes for jump to count at 100 metres past ramp.

Rocker
The natural bend in a ski (built in), as opposed to Flex.

Rooster tail
Plume in middle of wake thrown up by wake coming together.

Rudder
Another term for Fin.

Run
1 *Same as* Programme.
2 *A ski ride.*
3 *A* Pass *in slalom.*

Sequence
A set of tricks strung together in sequence.

Shortening
Normally accompanied by 1st, 2nd, 3rd, 4th, and so on, in slalom rope length.

Side curtain
See Apron.

Slalom
Skiing on slalom course.

Specialist
One-event skier. An overall skier can also specialise in one event.

Spin
To turn on trick skis. More spin needed for bigger tricks.

Spread
Similar problem/defect to Crush *except that skis spread.*

Spring
The same as Kick, Pop.

Step
A particular movement in tricks.

Tip
Front of a ski.

Toe-hold
1 *Attachment to trick handle for foot.*
2 *Name for trick done with foot in this attachment.*

Toe-strap
Same as Toe-hold (1).

Toe-turns
Same as Toe-holds (2).

Tow
A ski ride.

Towbar
Handle on tow-rope.

Track
The skis track when they bite or grip in the water.

Tricks
1 *Event of tricks.*
2 *Any individual tricks.*

Tunnel
Type of Concave, *running down ski like a narrow channel.*

Wake
Boat's path.

Wide
When rope is at right angles to boat's path in jumping.